Nehemiah

a 13-lesson study containing
weekly commentary
and
daily study questions

commentary on Lessons 2-13 by
Ray C. Stedman

commentary on Lesson 1 and
all daily study questions by
Nancy J. Collins

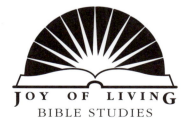

Published by Joy of Living Bible Studies
Printed in U.S.A.

For a free catalog please contact us at:

Joy of Living Bible Studies   800-999-2703 or 805-649-3307
P.O. Box 1377   website: www.joyofliving.org
Oak View, CA 93022   e-mail: info@joyofliving.org

The commentary portion of these lessons is based on a series of sermons given by Pastor Ray Stedman in 1989.

Unless otherwise noted, all Scripture quotations in these lessons are from the Holy Bible, *New International Version* (North American Edition). Copyright © 1973, 1978, 1984 by International Bible Society. Used by permission of Zondervan Publishing House.

Also quoted are:
Revised Standard Version of the Bible (RSV), copyrighted 1946 and 1952 by the Division of Christian Education of the NCCC, U.S.A., and used by permission.
King James Version (KJV)
1890 J.N. Darby Bible (DBY)
The Holy Bible: New King James Version (NKJV). Copyright © 1982 by Thomas Nelson, Inc. All rights reserved. Used by permission.

© Copyright 2002, Joy of Living Bible Studies, Inc. Box 1377, Oak View, CA 93022. All rights reserved.

Any omission of credits or permissions granted is unintentional. The publisher requests documentation for future printings.

ISBN 1-932017-01-1

About Joy of Living

For over 30 years Joy of Living has been effectively establishing individuals around the world in the sound, basic study of God's Word.

Evangelical and non-denominational, Joy of Living reaches across denominational and cultural barriers enriching lives through the simple pure truths of God's inspired Word, the Bible.

Studies are flexible, suited for both formal and informal meetings, as well as for personal study. Each lesson contains historical background, commentary and a week's worth of personal application questions, leading readers to discover fresh insights into God's Word. Courses covering many books in both the Old and New Testaments are available. Selected courses are also available in several foreign languages. Contact the Joy of Living office for details.

Joy of Living Bible Studies was founded by Doris W. Greig in 1971 and has grown to include classes in nearly every state in the Union and many foreign countries.

Contents

How to Use Joy of Living Materials   4

Lesson 1
Commentary: Introduction   5
Questions: Nehemiah 1   9

Lesson 2
Commentary: Nehemiah 1   13
Questions: Nehemiah 2   17

Lesson 3
Commentary: Nehemiah 2   21
Questions: Nehemiah 3   25

Lesson 4
Commentary: Nehemiah 3   29
Questions: Nehemiah 4-5   33

Lesson 5
Commentary: Nehemiah 4-5   37
Questions: Nehemiah 6-7   41

Lesson 6
Commentary: Nehemiah 6-7   45
Questions: Nehemiah 8   49

Lesson 7
Commentary: Nehemiah 8   53
Questions: Nehemiah 9   57

Lesson 8
Commentary: Nehemiah 9   61
Questions: Nehemiah 10   65

Lesson 9
Commentary: Nehemiah 10   69
Questions: Nehemiah 11:1—12:26   73

Lesson 10
Commentary: Nehemiah 11:1—12:26   77
Questions: Nehemiah 12:27-47   81

Lesson 11
Commentary: Nehemiah 12:27-47   85
Questions: Nehemiah 13:1-14   89

Lesson 12
Commentary: Nehemiah 13:1-14   93
Questions: Nehemiah 13:15-31   97

Lesson 13
Commentary: Nehemiah 13:15-31   101

How to Use Joy of Living Materials for Groups

This unique Bible study series may be used by people who know nothing about the Bible, as well as by more knowledgeable Christians. Many find a personal relationship with Jesus Christ as they study. Each person is nurtured and discipled in God's Word and in the small group.

Joy of Living is based on the idea that each person needs to open their Bible and let God speak to them by His Holy Spirit, to interpret the Scripture's message in relation to that person's needs and opportunities, in their family, church, job, community, and the world at large.

Only a Bible is needed for this study series. While commentaries may be helpful, it is not recommended that people consult them as they study. It is most important to let the Holy Spirit lead a person through the Bible passage and apply it to his or her heart and life.

In the first lesson of a series, the student receives an Introduction to the Bible book, plus the first week's daily study questions. Some questions are simple, and some are deeper for the more advanced student. The person works through the Bible passages each day, praying and asking God's guidance in applying the truth to their own life.

After the daily personal study of the passage, the students then go to a small group where they pray together and discuss what they have written in response to the questions about the passage, clarifying problem areas and getting more insight into the passage. The small group leader helps the group focus on the Bible's truth, and not just on discussing their own problems.

After groups meet for discussion and prayer, they often go to a large group meeting where a teacher gives a brief lecture covering the essential teaching of the Bible passage which was studied during the prior week and discussed in the small groups. The teacher may clarify the passage and challenge class members to live a more committed daily life.

At home, the student begins the next lesson, containing commentary notes on the prior week's passage and questions on a new Scripture passage.

Nehemiah
Lesson 1

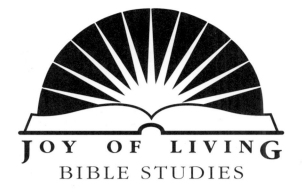

Introduction to Nehemiah

At first glance Nehemiah seems to be merely the story of the rebuilding of the walls of Jerusalem, but a closer look reveals the story of God's faithfulness to His people and His ability to restore not only a wall but people to a place of blessing.

God's Call, God's Promise
Genesis 11—35

Although Nehemiah takes place around the middle of the fifth century B.C., the story begins with one man over a thousand years earlier in the city of Ur of the Chaldees (see map, page 7). The descendants of Noah had spread out, multiplied and populated the earth and they had again abandoned the God who created them.

Yet God had not abandoned man. He called one man, Abram, and told him that if he would leave his country and go to a land God would show him, He would make of Abram a great nation, give him that land and through him all the world would be blessed. (It would be through his descendents that the Savior of the world would come.) In faith Abram (later called Abraham) obeyed God. Abraham had a son, Isaac, to whom the promise was given and he in turn had a son, Jacob, to whom the promise was given.

From a Family to a Nation
Genesis 46—Exodus 18

Jacob, whose name God changed to Israel, had 12 sons. When Jacob was an old man he, his sons and their families (70 people in all) went into Egypt to escape starvation during a great famine. One of the sons, Joseph, was already there and in great power. He was second only to the Pharaoh and because of this the family was well cared for.

However generations passed and the children of Israel grew in numbers. A new pharaoh arose and was fearful of this great number of people living within the borders of his land. To protect himself and his country he placed the Israelites in bondage where they remained for nearly 400 years.

As always God was faithful and in His time raised up a man named Moses. With great and mighty miracles God delivered the Israelites from the Egyptians and led them to the land He had promised to Abraham, Isaac and Jacob.

A Covenant Made — A Covenant Broken
Exodus 19 — 1 Samuel 7

Prior to entering the Promised Land, the general area of Israel today, God made a covenant with the Israelites. At Mount Sinai they agreed to serve the Lord and obey His commands. He gave them His Law and promised to bless them as long as they served Him. But even as God gave them His glorious Law they were rebelling against Him and worshipping other gods. And so began the cycle of God's blessing, Israel's rebellion, God's disciplining, their repentance, God's deliverance and blessing again.

The Israelites were told to drive the heathen nations from the land. They were to make no covenants with them, but they disobeyed and were led into idolatry by them.

The Kingdom
1 Samuel 8 — 2 Chronicles 36

Israel had the perfect government with the Lord Himself as King, and the Law of the Lord as the law of the land, yet they weren't satisfied. They wanted to be like the nations round about them. They wanted a man as their king. God granted their desire.

Saul, their first king, didn't fully obey the Lord so God gave the kingdom to David, a shepherd who loved the Lord. Although David made many mistakes, God said, "I have found David son of Jesse a man after my own heart" (Acts 13:22). God promised David that one of his descendants would have a kingdom without end. He was referring to Jesus Christ, the coming Savior, who would pay the price for the sins of the world and redeem mankind.

David's son Solomon inherited the kingdom from him, but because of Solomon's sin the kingdom was divided in the days of Solomon's son Rehoboam. The northern kingdom was known as Israel with Samaria as the capital. The southern kingdom was known as Judah with Jerusalem as the capital. As long as a godly king was on the throne the kingdoms tended to serve the Lord, but all too often there were ungodly kings and the people followed the practices of the heathen nations which included burning their children as sacrifices to the demonic god, Molech.

In His love and compassion God sent prophets to warn them to turn from their wickedness but with stiff necks and hard hearts they refused. So, after hundreds of years of rebellion and warnings the northern kingdom, Israel, was carried away into captivity (about 722 B.C.) by Assyria (2 Kings 17:6-18). As the people of Israel were taken away and settled in other lands, the king of Assyria brought people from other conquered nations and settled them in the land of Israel.

Except for brief periods of revival and despite seeing God's judgment fall upon the northern kingdom, the southern kingdom, Judah, continued in a path toward judgment and destruction, until finally a little over a hundred years later Judah was conquered by the Babylonians (2 Chronicles 36:6).

For Judah there were several deportations with opportunities for repentance in between, but they would not, as a nation, repent. We read in 2 Kings 24:13-14:

As the LORD had declared, Nebuchadnezzar removed all the treasures from the temple of the LORD and from the royal palace, and took away all the gold articles that Solomon king of Israel had made for the temple of the LORD. He carried into exile all Jerusalem: all the officers and fighting men, and all the craftsmen and artisans —a total of ten thousand. Only the poorest people of the land were left.

A Message of Hope – A Promise Made

But God does not abandon His people, nor does He leave them without hope. Even as the prophets were warning of judgment God had them prophesy a message of hope:

This is what the LORD says: "When seventy years are completed for Babylon, I will come to you and fulfill my gracious promise to bring you back to this place. For I know the plans I have for you," declares the LORD, "plans to prosper you and not to harm you, plans to give you hope and a future. Then you will call upon me and come and pray to me, and I will listen to you. You will seek me and find me when you seek me with all your heart. I will be found by you," declares the LORD, "and will bring you back from captivity. I will gather you from all the nations and places where I have banished you," declares the LORD, "and will bring you back to the place from which I carried you into exile." (Jeremiah 29:10-14)

A Promise Fulfilled
(Ezra — Nehemiah 1)

God was and is faithful. The Babylonians were conquered by the Persians and at the end of the 70 years prophesied by Jeremiah, Cyrus, king of Persia issued the following proclamation:

This is what Cyrus king of Persia says: "The LORD, the God of heaven, has given me all the kingdoms of the earth and he has appointed me to build a temple for him at Jerusalem in Judah. Anyone of his people among you —may his God be with him, and let him go up to Jerusalem in Judah and build the temple of the LORD, the God of Israel, the God who is in Jerusalem. And the people of any place where survivors may now be living are to provide him with silver and gold, with goods and livestock, and with freewill offerings for the temple of God in Jerusalem." (Ezra 1:1-4)

And so in 537 B.C. the Jews, led by Zerubabel, returned to the land of promise. As with any work of God, there was opposition, but God's promise held true— the temple in Jerusalem was rebuilt and sacrifice was restored. To keep the people from returning to the practices that caused God's judgment to fall on them, it would be necessary for them to know God's laws. In about 458 B.C. God raised up another man, a scribe named Ezra to lead another group back to Jerusalem. His desire was to teach God's law in Israel.

Thus the stage is set for Nehemiah. The scene switches to Susa, the capital of the Persian Empire where Nehemiah, a Jew, serves as cupbearer to the king. He knows of the rebuilding of the Temple, he knows that the sacrifices are being made and he knows of Ezra's journey and his desire to teach God's law. But Nehemiah also knows that the walls of Jerusalem have not been rebuilt and that leaves God's people vulnerable to those living round about them, those who were brought there by the Assyrians when the Jews were exiled, those who are not pleased that the Jews have returned. And so the story of Nehemiah begins.

A Hope for Us

God never abandons His people. He has promised us that He will never leave us or forsake us (Hebrews 13:5). God may have to discipline us or through our own actions we may fall into bondage to some sin. But because of what Jesus Christ has done for us by His sacrifice on the cross, God is always ready to forgive and restore us to a place of blessing. Not only does He desire to bless us but He wants to rebuild the walls of our lives and teach us His ways so that we don't fall into sin and bondage again.

Nehemiah is a message of hope and restoration. What God did for them, He will do for us. He will take the broken places of our lives and rebuild them for our protection and His glory.

Jesus Christ is the same, yesterday, today and forever. (Hebrews 13:8)

Nehemiah Lesson 1

Where Nehemiah took place

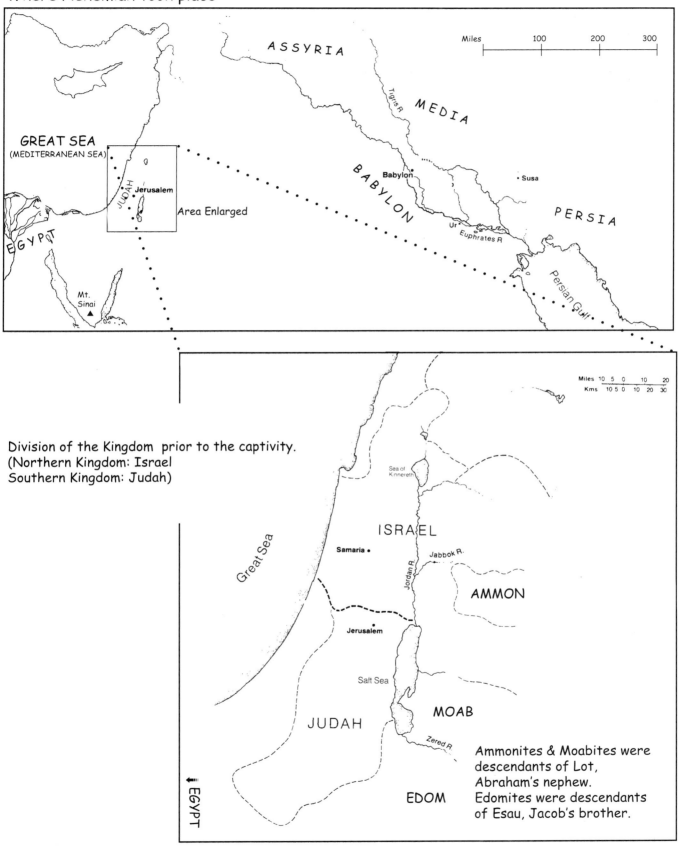

Division of the Kingdom prior to the captivity.
(Northern Kingdom: Israel
Southern Kingdom: Judah)

Ammonites & Moabites were descendants of Lot, Abraham's nephew. Edomites were descendants of Esau, Jacob's brother.

Maps adapted from *Reproducible Maps, Charts, TimeLines & Illustrations*, published by Regal Books. Used by permission.

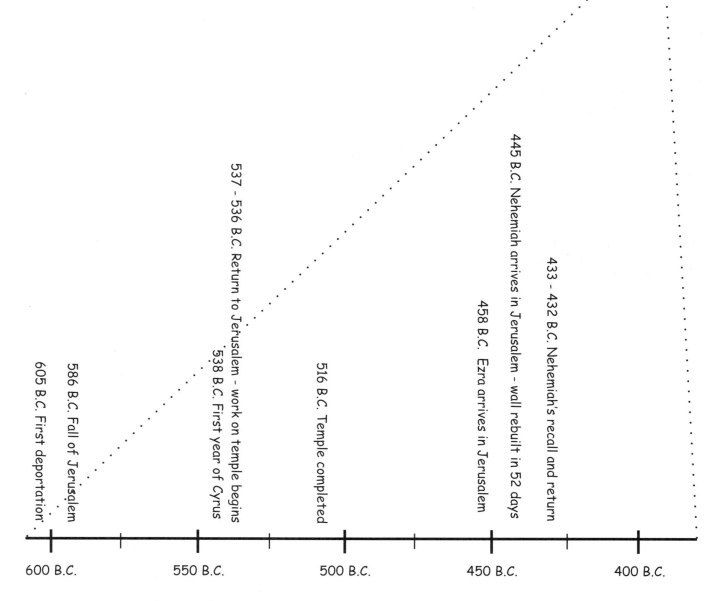

Approximate dates for events relating to the return of the exiles, the rebuilding of the Temple and the eventual rebuilding of the wall of Jerusalem.

Nehemiah Lesson 1

Study Questions

Before you begin each day:
    a. Pray and ask God to speak to you through His Holy Spirit.
    b. Do not use other source books for your answers.
    c. Write your answers and the verses you used.
    d. Remember that the challenge questions are for those who have the time or inclination to do them.
    e. Personal questions are to be shared with the class only if you wish to share.
    f. If you desire, insert your name in the assigned verses to make them more personal.

First Day: Read the Commentary.

1. What meaningful or new thought did you find in the notes on the Introduction to Nehemiah, or from your teacher's lecture? What personal application did you choose to apply to your life?

2. Look for a verse in the lesson to memorize this week. Write it down, carry it with you, tack it to your bulletin board, on the dashboard of your car, etc. Make a real effort to learn the verse and its "address" (reference of where it is found in the Bible).

Second Day: Read all of Nehemiah 1, concentrating on verses 1-2.

1. Nehemiah was written in the twentieth year of the reign of King Artaxerxes (see Nehemiah 1:1 and 2:1). Who wrote this book according to Nehemiah 1:1?

2. Where is he writing from? Locate this on the map on page 7.

3. Who was Nehemiah questioning and where had they come from? (See Nehemiah 1:2.) Locate this on the map. Note the distance it is from Susa.

4. What did Nehemiah want to know? (See Nehemiah 1:2.)

5. Personal: Like Nehemiah, is there anyone you are concerned about? Maybe you haven't heard from them for awhile. Pray for them right now. Write them a note or give them a phone call and let them know you are thinking of them and praying for them.

Third Day: Read all of Nehemiah 1, concentrating on verse 3.

1. In Nehemiah 1:3 who is in great trouble and disgrace?

2. Prior to the Israelites entering the Promised Land (around 1000 years before the writing of Nehemiah), what warning did God give them in Deuteronomy 4:24-27, and what would be the consequence if they didn't heed the warning?

3. a. Challenge: Read 2 Chronicles 36:14-21. Describe what happened to Judah and why. (This was about 150 years before Nehemiah.)

   b. Re-read 2 Chronicles 36:15-16. Had God warned them and given them opportunity to change their ways? What was their response?

4. a. Read Jeremiah 29:10-15. This was written to the Jews in captivity. What was God's attitude toward His people even when He had to discipline them? See verses 10-11.

   b. What attitude would God's people develop toward Him while in captivity? (See Jeremiah 29:12-13.)

   c. What promises did God give His people in Jeremiah 29:12-14?

5. a. According to Nehemiah 1:3, did God fulfill His promise to bring back His people from exile?

   b. Personal: God always keeps His promises. What encouragement does this give you?

6. a. Read Hebrews 12:6-10. Who does God discipline and why? (See verses 6 and 10.)

Nehemiah Lesson 1

b. Personal: Has God ever had to discipline you? Write Jeremiah 29:11 inserting your own name.

Fourth Day: Read all of Nehemiah 1, concentrating on verses 3-7.

1. What was the condition of those who had survived the exile and were back in Judah? See Nehemiah 1:3a.

2. Why were the people in trouble and disgrace? See Nehemiah 1:3b.

3. Walls were a defense for a city and the gates were what allowed access to and exit from the city. According to Nehemiah 1:6-7, what had brought about this destruction of their defense?

4. What were Nehemiah's first steps to remedy the problem? See Nehemiah 1:4.

5. a. Personal: Have the protective walls of your life been damaged, perhaps by sin and disobedience to God? Think about it carefully, and write your thoughts here.

   b. Read James 4:8-10. What actions are you to take if you have sinned?

   c. What promises does God give you in these verses?

   d. Write a prayer thanking God for these promises.

Fifth Day: Read all of Nehemiah 1, concentrating on verses 8-9.

1. Whose promise is Nehemiah trusting in and what is promised in verses 8-9?

2. Challenge: Read Numbers 23:19 and Hebrews 6:18-19. What do they say about the character of God and the surety of His Word?

3. In Genesis 3:1-7 Adam and Eve chose not to believe and obey God and ate the fruit of the Tree of the Knowledge of Good and Evil. Read Romans 5:12. What happened because Adam didn't believe God?

4. What does God's Word tell us in Romans 5:8-9?

5. Personal: Read Romans 10:9-10. Do you believe what God has said? If so write a prayer telling Him that you believe that Jesus Christ died to take away your sins. Be certain to thank Him. Now tell someone that you believe God and have put your trust in Him.

Sixth Day: Read all of Nehemiah 1, concentrating on verses 9-11.

1. What action did God's people need to take? See Nehemiah 1:9.

2. Who was Nehemiah praying for? (See verse 10.)

3. To whom did Nehemiah want God to listen? (See verse 11.)

4. What do each of the following verses say about whom God does and does not listen to?

   Psalms 66:18

   Proverbs 15:29

   John 9:31

   James 4:3

   James 5:16b

5. Personal: If there are areas of your life that aren't right, do like Nehemiah did and confess them to the Lord (see Nehemiah 1:6-7). This is the first step toward restoration. Write 1 John 1:9 inserting your own name.

Nehemiah
Lesson 2

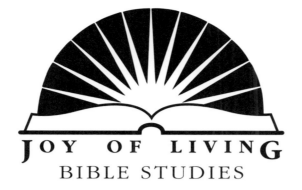

Don't Despair — Begin To Repair

We are beginning studies in the Old Testament book of Nehemiah. There are three Old Testament books, Ezra, Nehemiah, and Esther, which belong together for they cover in general the same period of time, after the Babylonian captivity when Israel had returned to Jerusalem and had begun again the worship of *Jehovah* in the restored temple.

Ezra and Nehemiah are one book in the Hebrew Bible. Ezra, the priest, led an early return to Israel and restored worship in the rebuilt temple in Jerusalem. The prophets Haggai and Zechariah had ministered to the people before that time and had urged them to build the temple, and Ezra went back to restore the worship of that temple. Nehemiah, who was a contemporary of Ezra, led a later return. He was a layman, a butler to the Emperor, Artaxerxes I of Persia, which is now the modern nation of Iran.

Nehemiah is the story of the rebuilding of the walls of Jerusalem, which took place in the fifth century before Christ. It is part of the long history of that troubled city which today is still in the news, and still in trouble, as you well know. This ancient city is still surrounded by thick walls, but they are not the same walls that Nehemiah built. Those walls have disappeared, and the walls that are there now are of a much later date. However, I was in Jerusalem in 1983, and I vividly remember standing one day in company with the famous Israeli archaeologist, Avigad, on top of a section of wall which he told us, with great enthusiasm and pride, he had clearly established as part of the wall that Nehemiah built. This book, therefore, is an historic account of the rebuilding of the walls of that great city.

But Nehemiah did more than rebuild a wall, as we will learn. This book is also the story of the restoring of a people from ruin and despair to a new walk with God. Jerusalem is not only an historic city which has for centuries been the center of the life of the nation of Israel (and, in fact, the center of the biblical record), it is also a symbolic city. Jerusalem is also used in a pictorial sense throughout the scriptures. What it pictures is the place where God desires to dwell. When the city was first designated to King David as the place where God wanted him to build the temple, he was told that this was the place where God would dwell among His people. Jerusalem therefore, throughout the Old and New Testaments, has pictured the place where God seeks to dwell. However, it is only a picture — it is not the actual place where God dwells for, according to the New Testament, man is to be the dwelling place of God. God seeks to dwell in the human spirit. That is the great secret that humanity has largely lost today, but which New Testament Christianity seeks to restore. The Apostle Paul's great statement in the letter to the Colossians is, "Christ in you, the hope of glory" (Colossians 1:27). This is God's provision and desire for man.

Jerusalem in ruins, therefore, is a picture of a life that has lost its defenses against attack and lies open to repeated hurt and misery. If you are at all acquainted with the world in which we live today, you will know that every time you turn your television on you are exposed to the hurt and misery of people whose walls have been broken down. Jerusalem in ruins is a vivid picture of their danger and despair. The book of Nehemiah depicts the way of recovery from breakdown and ruin to a condition of peace, security, restored order, and usefulness.

A New Beginning

The book of Nehemiah is the story of a new beginning. Traditionally, New Year's Day is the day on which we review our lives. We examine our walls and our gates, as it were, reflecting on the damage and destruction that may have occurred, and we resolve to do better in the New Year. This practice of making New Year's resolutions has largely fallen out of style, however. It used to be quite common, but it has fallen into neglect. People break their resolutions so quickly they have given up making them, or else they have gone in for rather foolish, silly things, like giving up eating ice cream in bed, or wearing overshoes, or something else easy to do or to stop.

I read of a survey taken of 200 people who had made New Year's resolutions, sincerely resolving to do better in certain areas of their lives. But the survey revealed that by the end of January half of them had broken their resolutions entirely, and none of the 200 made it through the first year! This would probably be the same story for most of us. The reason is, when you resolve to do better you are depending upon your own willpower to carry it through — and will power is what most of us lack. We find it more comfortable to go back to the old habits.

In Nehemiah we learn the reason why it is difficult to keep New Year's resolutions, why there is so much failure in this area. It is because, if I may put it very clearly right at the beginning, there is no recognition of God as a necessary part of the process! The most widespread secular illusion of our day is that we do not need God to do what we want to do. We think we can function quite adequately without Him. It is amazing to me how many Christians live on that basis. I find in my own life tendencies to depend upon myself to do certain things and to ignore the need for God in this process. The book of Nehemiah is designed to teach us that only with God's help can we actually change ourselves and recover from the damage and ruin of the past. That is the central lesson of this book.

During the past we have all heard of the moral difficulties and failures of prominent television evangelists and Christian leaders. We have seen the moral collapse of outstanding and prominent leaders. Among them was a man who was widely respected. He was not a flamboyant sensationalist, like certain of the television evangelists. He was a very widely respected, godly man. To everyone's horror and surprise it was learned that he had fallen into adultery. When it was made public he had to leave the work in which he was involved. He spent over a year in a state of self-imposed exile, seeking to restore his relationships with his wife and family. He has written an account of his recovery and I would like to share with you a quotation from that book in which he describes an incident during the time of his recovery. He writes:

In one of the darkest hours of my broken-world condition, I found myself one day in the front row of a Dallas church where I had been asked to give a talk. I had made a long-term commitment to be there, but had it not been for my hosts' hard work of preparation, I would have tried to cancel my participation. Frankly, I was in no mood to speak to anyone. But I felt constrained not to cancel, and so there I was.

When the service began, a group of young men and women took places at the front of the congregation and began to lead with instruments and voices in a chain of songs and hymns: some contemporary, others centuries old. As we moved freely from melody to melody, I became aware of a transformation in my inner world. I was being strangely lifted by the music and its content of thankfulness and celebration. If my heart had been heavy, the hearts of others about me were apparently light because, together, we seemed to rise in spirit, the music acting much like the thermal air currents that lift an eagle or a hawk high above the earth.

I not only felt myself rising out of the darkness of my spirit, but I felt as if I were being bathed, washed clean. And as the gloom melted away, a quiet joy and a sense of cleansing swept in and took its place. I felt free to express my turbulent emotions with tears. The congregation's praise was a therapy of the spirit: indescribable in its power. It was a day I shall never forget. No one in that sanctuary knew how high they had lifted one troubled man far above his broken-world anguish. Were there others there that day feeling as I did? Perhaps they would have affirmed as I did: God was there.[1]

That is the difference that a recognition of God makes in recovering from anguish and ruin.

Nehemiah's Diary

With that I would like to turn to Nehemiah's diary, the memoirs of a man who was used of God to lead a whole city to recovery:

The words of Nehemiah son of Hacaliah:

In the month of Kislev [that is December] in the twentieth year [i.e., of Artaxerxes], while I was in the citadel of Susa [the winter capital of Persia], Hanani, one of my brothers, came from Judah with some other men, and I questioned them about the Jewish remnant that survived the exile, and also about Jerusalem.

They said to me, "Those who survived the exile and are back in the province are in great trouble and disgrace. The wall of Jerusalem is broken down, and its gates have been burned with fire." (Nehemiah 1:1-3)

Notice the description of Jerusalem. The people were in trouble. They were feeling a great sense of disgrace and reproach. The walls of the city were broken down (Nebuchadnezzar had started that many years earlier). The gates had been burned with fire and were no longer usable. If we take Jerusalem as a symbol of our own lives, there are many people who fit this description.

Look Back on Your Life

You look back on your life and you see there are places where the walls have been broken down. There is no longer any ability left to resist destructive attacks. You have fallen victim to sinful habits that you now find difficult, if not impossible, to break. That is the kind of ruin that is described here.

There may be some who feel unable to stop wrongful sexual practices. You have gone along with the ways of the world. You have fallen into practices that the Bible says are wrong. You know they are wrong. But you have difficulty stopping them. You may be indulging in pornography. I am amazed at the number of Christians who secretly indulge themselves in this area. You may be addicted to drugs. You

Nehemiah Lesson 2

may be hooked on tobacco or alcohol. Perhaps you have a bitter spirit. You can be an addict of a critical, censorious attitude that complains about everything as much as you can be an addict to drugs. It is so habitual that you find yourself having difficulty stopping it. Perhaps your drift began innocently. You did not realize you were forming a habit, but now you no longer can stop it. Your defenses are gone. The walls of your city are broken down. Perhaps also your gates are burned. Gates are ways in and out. They are the way by which other people get to know you as you really are. Perhaps your gates have been destroyed, again by wrong habits.

Perhaps you were sexually abused as a child. This phenomenon seems to be surfacing more and more frequently in our day. The shame of it, and the scarring of it, has kept you a recluse. Your gates are burned and nobody has access to you. Perhaps you were a victim of divorce — or rape — or of some bitter experience — and you feel betrayed or sabotaged.

You want to run and hide. No one can reach you. You have been so badly burned you are now touchy and inaccessible. There are parts of your life you cannot talk about. You do not want anyone to know. You have a sense of great personal distress and are feeling reproach and disgrace. Your have been scarred emotionally.

No one may know about it. To others you appear to be a success. They think you are doing fine, but inwardly you know you are not. As you examine the walls and the gates of your life you find much of it in ruins. How do you handle that?

That is the great question many face. But this is where the Bible comes in. That is why the scriptures are given to us. The men and women of the past have been through these self-same difficulties and they have told us how to handle them. This great book of Nehemiah is one of the most helpful pictures we have of how to recover from broken lives — "broken-world anguish."

Steps to Recovery

The steps that Nehemiah took cover seven chapters of this book. They are very specific steps, very orderly — and very effective! Taken in order they will lead to a full recovery of usefulness. We are only going to examine the first step in this lesson. We find it in these words,

When I heard these things, I sat down and wept. For some days I mourned and fasted and prayed before the God of Heaven. (Nehemiah 1:4)

Nehemiah clearly has a deep sense of personal concern. He is willing to face the facts, to weep over them, and tell God about them. That is always the place to begin. There is nothing superficial about this. A popular song once said, "Don't worry, Be happy." But that is mere salve over a deep cancer. What is needed is an honest facing of the ruin, whatever it may be, and, without blaming or attempting to involve somebody else, tell it all to God. By yourself, alone, face the facts. Take all the time you want and pour it out before God. Weep, if you feel like it. Tell Him all the hurt, the fear, and the pain. That is always the place to start, according to scripture. A broken spirit and a contrite heart God always welcomes (see Psalm 51:17).

I would suggest that you follow the pattern of Nehemiah's prayer. We will not spend a lot of time with this, but I will quickly point out the four specific things Nehemiah did in this marvelous prayer recorded here:

First, he recognized the character of God:

Oh LORD, God of heaven, the great and awesome God, who keeps his covenant of love with those who love Him and obey his commands, let your ear be attentive and your eyes open to hear the prayer your servant is praying before you day and night for your servants, the people of Israel. (Nehemiah 1:5b-6a)

The ruin you are concerned with may not always be yours personally. It may be that of someone close to you whose life you see falling apart because of certain habits or attitudes they have allowed to enter their experience. You feel like Nehemiah, and you want to weep and mourn and tell God about it. That is always the place to start, for God is a responsive God. He gives attention to the prayers of His people. And He is a God of power and ability, and, above all, a God of love.

The second thing Nehemiah did was he repented of all personal and corporate sins:

I confess the sins we Israelites, including myself and my father's house, have committed against you. We have acted very wickedly toward you. We have not obeyed the commands, decrees and laws you gave your servant Moses. (Nehemiah 1:6b-7)

This is an honest facing of his own guilt. Notice the absence of self-righteousness. He does not say, "Lord, I am thinking of those terrible sinners back there in Jerusalem. Be gracious to them because they have fallen into wrong actions." No, he puts himself into this picture, saying, "I have contributed to this problem. There are things that I did or did not do that have made this ruin possible. I confess before you, Lord, the sins of myself and my father's house." There is no attempt to excuse or to blame others for this. It is a simple acknowledgment of wrong.

It has always been true of the people of God that any degree of self-justification will cancel out recovery. If you try to excuse yourself for what is wrong in your life, you block your own recovery. Just admit it, declare it. This is exactly contrary to the spirit of the age in which we live, but this is God's way and it is the first step in the process of recovery.

Then, third, Nehemiah reminded God of His gracious promises:

Remember the instruction you gave your servant Moses, saying, "If you are unfaithful, I will scatter you among the nations, but if you return to me and obey my commands, then even if your exiled people are at the farthest horizon, I will gather them from there and bring them to the place I have chosen as a dwelling for my Name."

They are your servants and your people, whom you redeemed by your great strength and your mighty hand. (Nehemiah 1:8-10)

Nehemiah reminds himself of the nature of God: He is a God of forgiveness, a God of restoration, a God of great power. When the heart is right, God can change all the external circumstances of a situation and make it entirely different. And He will do so. He promises He will!

Only once in the history of the world has there been a prediction made of the entire history of a nation. It is found in the book of Deuteronomy, chapters 28-30. There, in a marvelous message, Moses prophetically outlines the entire history of Israel. He said they would disobey God; they would be scattered among the nations; they would go into exile. But if there they would turn again and acknowledge their evil, God would restore them and bring them back to the land. Nehemiah reminds God of that wonderfully gracious promise.

Even the prodigal son in Jesus' story in the New Testament, languishing in the far country, eating pig's food, reminds himself that his last resort is, "I will arise and go [back] to my father" (Luke 15:18a KJV). When he comes back, to his great surprise, he finds his father with open arms ready to receive him.

The fourth thing Nehemiah did was he requested specific help to begin this process:

O Lord, let your ear be attentive to the prayer of this your servant and to the prayer of your servants who delight in revering your name. [There were others praying with him.] Give your servant success today by granting him favor in the presence of this man. (Nehemiah 1:11a)

What man? He goes on to tell us:

I was cup-bearer to the king. (Nehemiah 1:11b)

He had a place to start. It was not going to be easy, but he knew what he had to do. It was going to take the authority of the top power in the whole empire (in fact in the whole world of that day). That is not easy to arrange. Talk about playing politics! You really have to maneuver to get a king, an emperor over a vast domain, to do what you want to do, especially when there are elements involved that are threatening to him personally. That is what Nehemiah foresaw. But he believes that God will help him. And so he starts to pray, and ask for grace and strength to carry out the steps that are necessary to begin recovery.

No matter what the ruin of any life may be there is always a place to start. There is a place where you must begin. You need to apologize to someone. You need to go to somebody and straighten something out. You need to stop some practice that is wrong. You need to open yourself up to counsel. You need to seek advice. You need to get some guidance. There is always a first step. That is where you must begin.

And whatever you pray, pray that God will give you the grace, the strength and the determination to take that step. Then, the process of recovery has begun.

Let me close by asking this very personal question: Do you want to be a better man or woman? Do you long to be free from old habits, old attitudes, old practices, old and perhaps harmful friends? Then start here:

* Take stock of your life.
* Examine your walls and your gates.
* Do business with God.

Prayer

Thank you, Father, for this wonderfully practical book which sets out a safe guideline to recovery and usefulness. Thank you that when we fall and go astray to any degree, you do not leave us there; you make a way back. We pray that many today will be determined to begin where Nehemiah began: to tell the whole story in your ear and thus begin the process of recovery. We ask this in Jesus' name. Amen.

Notes
1. McDonald, Gordon. *Rebuilding Your Broken World.*

Nehemiah Lesson 2   17

Study Questions

Before you begin each day:
   a. Pray and ask God to speak to you through His Holy Spirit.
   b. Do not use other source books for your answers.
   c. Write your answers and the verses you used.
   d. Remember that the challenge questions are for those who have the time or inclination to do them.
   e. Personal questions are to be shared with the class only if you wish to share.
   f. If you desire, insert your name in the assigned verses to make them more personal.

First Day: Read the Commentary on Nehemiah 1.

1. What meaningful or new thought did you find in the notes on Nehemiah 1, or from your teacher's lecture? What personal application did you choose to apply to your life?

2. Look for a verse in the lesson to memorize this week. Write it down, carry it with you, tack it to your bulletin board, on the dashboard of your car, etc. Make a real effort to learn the verse and its "address" (reference of where it is found in the Bible).

Second Day: Read all of Nehemiah 2, concentrating on verses 1-2.

1. Four months had passed since Nehemiah had heard the report and begun praying about the condition of Jerusalem and those who had returned from the exile. From Nehemiah 2:1-2, how do you think Nehemiah was feeling about Jerusalem and the exiles?

2. What does Matthew 7:7-8 say about prayer?

3. Read Luke 18:1. What attitude does Jesus tell His disciples to have concerning prayer?

4. a. Read Hebrews 10:35-36. What does verse 35 say is the result of our confidence in the Lord?

   b. What are we exhorted to do in verse 36 to obtain what God has promised?

5. a. Although saddened by the situation in Jerusalem, Nehemiah continued to be faithful to God. Our feelings do not have to get in the way of our faith. Regardless of how you feel, choose to believe God. Read Hebrews 6:12. What two things are needed in order to inherit what has been promised?

18   Joy of Living Bible Studies

b. Personal: Is there a particular area of your life where you need to simply trust God and wait for Him to answer? Write a prayer now asking God to help you to persevere and wait for His answer

Third Day: Read all of Nehemiah 2, concentrating on verses 1-4.

1. What does verse 1 say about Nehemiah's attitude while performing his duties?

2. a. Read Ephesians 6:5-7. What attitude should slaves (or employees) have toward those who have authority over them? (See verse 5.)

   b. When should you have this attitude? (See Ephesians 6:6.)

   c. Explain how our service or work should be done, according to Ephesians 6:7.

3. Read 1 Corinthians 10:31. What should our purpose be in everything that we do?

4. a. Read Philippians 2:14-15. As believers, what should our attitude be in everything we do? (See verse 14.)

   b. Why should we have this attitude? (See Philippians 2:15.)

5. a. Challenge: Do you think Nehemiah's attitude may have influenced the king's response to him?

   b. Personal: Do you ever have trouble with your attitude? Do you sometimes murmur and complain about what you have to do, your circumstances or those around you? Ask God to forgive you and to change your attitude. Write Philippians 2:13-15 here, inserting your own name.

Fourth Day: Read all of Nehemiah 2, concentrating on verses 2-8.

1. From Nehemiah 2:2, how did Nehemiah feel when the king questioned him?

Nehemiah Lesson 2

2. What does Psalm 56:3 say we should do when we are afraid?

3. What did Nehemiah do in Nehemiah 2:4 that shows he was trusting the Lord?

4. Did Nehemiah ask for what he wanted? (See Nehemiah 2:5.) Do you think he had thought this out during the months he was waiting and praying?

5. According to Proverbs 21:1, who directs the heart of the king (or those in authority)?

6. Did God finally answer Nehemiah's prayer? Who did God use to answer his prayers? See Nehemiah 2:6-8.

7. a. Nehemiah trusted the Lord. He prayed and waited. Then, just prior to answering the king, Nehemiah again called on the Lord and acknowledged Him. Write Proverbs 3:5-6 in your own words.

   b. Personal: How can you apply this principle to your own life?

Fifth Day: Read all of Nehemiah 2, concentrating on verses 9-16.

1. How did the non-Jewish rulers of those living in the land respond to Nehemiah's arrival? (See Nehemiah 2:10.)

2. At first did Nehemiah tell anyone what God had put in his heart to do for Jerusalem? (See Nehemiah 2:12.)

3. What did Nehemiah do before speaking to the Jews, priests, nobles, rulers and the rest who would do the work? (See Nehemiah 2:11-15.)

4. In Nehemiah 2:17 what does Nehemiah ask them to do and why?

20   Joy of Living Bible Studies

5. a. What information did Nehemiah add in Nehemiah 2:18 that might have influenced their response?

    b. What was their response?

6. a. Personal: Are there areas of your life that, like the walls of Jerusalem, need to be rebuilt? Take a few moments and, like Nehemiah, make a list of those areas.

    b. Personal: Now, take that list to the Lord in prayer. Ask Him to show you if there are steps you need to take to begin rebuilding those areas of your life. Perhaps you need to forgive, or ask forgiveness of someone. Be willing to take those steps and, like Nehemiah's workers, "begin the good work."

Sixth Day: Read all of Nehemiah 2, concentrating on verses 19-20.

1. What did the enemy do when they heard what God's people were planning to do?

2. Why does Nehemiah say they will have success?

3. Who will do the rebuilding?

4. What share or right do their enemies have in Jerusalem?

5. Personal: When you decide to rebuild the broken areas of your life, the enemy of your soul may make fun of you or accuse you. But if you have accepted Jesus Christ as your Savior, you are God's child, and God has given you many promises about restoring you and making you whole. Write Hebrews 13:20-21 here, inserting your own name.

Nehemiah Lesson 3

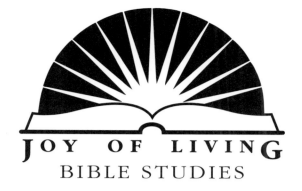

JOY OF LIVING BIBLE STUDIES

Don't Hesitate — Investigate!

We have in English a number of proverbs that urge us to action when the time is right. Shakespeare wrote, "There is a tide in the affairs of men, which taken at the flood, leads on to fortune." In the days when blacksmiths were common, we used to hear the proverb, "Strike while the iron is hot." Today we have shortened it to: "Get with it!"

In the second chapter of Nehemiah we come to just such a moment. In the last lesson we left our hero weeping and praying over the ruins of Jerusalem, beseeching God to lead him in a program of recovery. In the wonderful way the Bible has, this is intended to illustrate the damaged and ruined areas of our lives that need to be rebuilt, repaired or recovered. As we pursue that interpretation through Nehemiah, we shall find much practical help on how to reclaim a ruined life.

Many today find themselves in almost total ruin. They have lost their way and are wide open to the attacks of any destructive or hostile force. Others have severely damaged areas in their lives. They are, perhaps, still held in bondage to wrongful attitudes or habits. It almost goes without saying that if you are praying for help, as Nehemiah prayed for help in the opening chapter of this book, then you should expect an answer:

* Expect God to do something.
* Be ready for it when it comes.

An opportunity to change will surely appear, at times rather unexpectedly or after a longer period of time than you think it ought to take, but it will happen because the God we worship is a God who answers prayer.

Persevere in Prayer

We find Nehemiah at that point of opportunity:

In the month of Nisan in the twentieth year of King Artaxerxes, when wine was brought for him, I took the wine and gave it to the king. I had not been sad in his presence before; so the king asked me, "Why does your face look so sad when you are not ill? This can be nothing but sadness of heart."

I was very much afraid, but I said to the king, "May the king live forever! Why should my face not look sad when the city where my fathers are buried lies in ruins, and its gates have been destroyed by fire?" The king said to me, "What is it you want?" Then I prayed to the God of heaven.

(Nehemiah 2:1-4)

Notice that this chapter has a different date than the opening words of chapter 1. It is in the month of Nisan of the Hebrew calendar when Nehemiah finally has an opportunity to inform the king of his concern over Jerusalem. In lesson 2 we looked at incidents that took place in the month of Kislev, which is approximately the same as our month of December. Nisan corresponds to our April, so there is a lapse of about four months between these chapters. We are not told why Nehemiah delayed that long in bringing his problem to the king. But we can presume that because he was a man of prayer he was waiting for the Lord to indicate the right time. Suddenly, in Nisan, that time came.

God often works in lives this way today. We are hasty, impatient creatures. We want our prayers answered tomorrow, or even yesterday! We pray, and we expect God's answer right away. But God often delays His answers. It is not because He is impotent or unwilling. There is much teaching in scripture that a delayed answer does not indicate an unwilling God. We are taught again and again in scripture to persevere in prayer — to keep praying till the answer comes. Evidently Nehemiah has been doing this and the indication of it is that his heart is still deeply troubled over the state of Jerusalem. So much so that when he comes before the king in the performance of his normal duties of serving the wine, his face shows his concern. This is the first time he had ever allowed it to appear but apparently his concern is so great it breaks through his control. The king notices this immediately and asks him why he is so sad. Nehemiah tells us that his response to that question was: "I was very much afraid."

That may sound strange to us for it looks as though the king is simply being solicitous here. He seems truly concerned about the welfare of a trusted and beloved servant, and he is quite naturally inquiring about the cause. But Nehemiah's fear has a sound basis. He was the cupbearer, remember. It was his responsibility to taste the king's wine before it was served to make sure that no one had poisoned it. In those days of totalitarian monarchs, assassination was the only way one could be removed from office. The usual method was to poison his food or his wine. This was a dangerous job Nehemiah had. It is obvious that he had to be a man of unlimited integrity and trustworthiness. The king relied upon him to keep him safe. He must be always above suspicion, keeping the king's trust at all times. If the king grew suspicious or distrustful, Nehemiah's life would be in danger. He would not only lose his job, but he could also lose his head. That is why he was "very much afraid." But Nehemiah was just such a man as the job required. He was trustworthy and thoroughly reliable.

Though this is a moment of danger, it is also one of great opportunity. This is God's open door. Nehemiah's response is to shoot up a prayer to heaven for help. In his thoughts, without words, he formulated a quick plea for help, and then made his response.

Be Ready

...and I answered the king, "If it pleases the king and if your servant has found favor in his sight, let him send me to the city in Judah where my fathers are buried so that I can rebuild it." Then the king, with the queen sitting beside him, asked me, "How long will your journey take, and when will you get back?" It pleased the king to send me; so I set a time.

I also said to him, "If it pleases the king, may I have letters to the governors of Trans-Euphrates [the provinces on the west of the river], so that they will provide me safe-conduct until I arrive in Judah? And may I have a letter to Asaph, keeper of the king's forest, so he will give me timber to make beams for the gates of the citadel by the temple and for the city wall and for the residence I will occupy?" And because the gracious hand of my God was upon me, the king granted my requests. (Nehemiah 2:5-8)

Observe how tactful is Nehemiah's presentation. Twice he refers to Jerusalem, not as the capital of Judah, or even by its name, for it had a reputation as a troublesome city and had been the source of revolt in the empire before, but he designates it as "the city where my fathers are buried." That is an accommodation to the emperor's own concerns. These ancient kings were greatly concerned about their burial. They expended vast amounts of labor and money on their memorials. This king would be immediately sympathetic to Nehemiah's desire to go and restore the city where his fathers were buried.

Note also the thoroughness with which he had thought out all that he would need. He knew it would require a lengthy period of time, so he asked for the time he needed, and whatever he asked for he was granted that amount.

In parenthesis, as it were, Nehemiah says that he asked the king, "with the queen sitting beside him." Some Bible scholars think this queen might well have been Queen Esther. She was a Jewess and would be very interested in restoring the site of Jerusalem. Other scholars feel that Esther's reign came before this time, though Esther may have been the mother-in-law of the queen who is mentioned here, and therefore had some influence upon this queen and, through her, upon king Artaxerxes.

Not only did Nehemiah need sufficient time for this expedition, but he needed secure travel. So he asked for letters to the governors of the provinces that he would have to pass through, to provide safe conduct for him. We learn later in this book that this not only gave him diplomatic immunity, but it also meant that he was appointed as the governor of the province of Judah. From secular sources we learn that there had been trouble in the province of Syria (just north of Judah), two years earlier. The satrap (governor) of that province had rebelled against Artaxerxes. It is likely that the king welcomed this opportunity to place a trusted man in the governorship of Judah and interpose a buffer between Syria and Egypt who were often at war in those days. Thus this proposed journey of Nehemiah was something the king found very satisfying.

Finally, Nehemiah knew he would need some special supplies which only the king's authority could provide. He asked for special timbers to be cut for him out of the king's forest. Nehemiah got what he asked for. He had done his homework thoroughly.

This suggests to us that if we are truly concerned about rebuilding parts of our life, we need to think seriously about what it will require. We must assess what we will actually need, what steps we should take, and what may be involved in changing our habits so that we can be freed to be what God wants us to be. Nehemiah teaches us that we need to face honestly our situation.

Confident in God's Power

In verses 9-10, we get the account of his journey.

So I went to the governors of Trans-Euphrates and gave them the king's letters. The king had also sent army officers and cavalry with me. When Sanballat the Horonite and Tobiah the Ammonite official heard about this, they were very much disturbed that someone had come to promote the welfare of the Israelites.

(Nehemiah 2:9-10)

This was an impressive array. I know what a difference it makes to have a military escort. Several years ago, when I was in Israel, I was driving from Galilee back to Jerusalem through what is now known as the West Bank. In those days it was much less tense than it is today. On the way I picked up three sub-machine-gun carrying Israeli soldiers who were hitchhiking. I drove them down into the city of Nablus, which is the major city of the West Bank. Just south of that is the little village of Sychar, where Jacob's well is located, I asked them if they would like to visit it with me, and found — to my amazement — that though they were stationed just outside the city they had not known that Jacob's well was located there. We went up to the gate and knocked on it. It was at the noon hour when the site was normally closed, but the Syrian priest in charge of it came to the gate. When he saw me with three armed soldiers behind me, he flung the gate open and took me on a tour of all the premises! He really rolled out the carpet! So I know

Nehemiah Lesson 3

from personal experience that an armed escort makes a great impression and commands immediate attention.

Nehemiah not only came with a full military escort but it is apparent from this account that he came with the full authority of the throne of Persia behind him. I want you to remember that if you set out to change something in your life for the better, you have the full authority of the throne of God behind you; you may proceed with full confidence that the unseen, but very real, power of God is backing you up!

Nehemiah met two very troublesome enemies when he got there: Sanballat the Horonite, and Tobiah the Ammonite. An Horonite is a devotee of the god Horon, a local deity of Palestine. This indicates this man was a pagan. Tobiah was a citizen of Ammon, which was one of the tribes descended from Lot, the nephew of Abraham, and thus related to Israel but always an enemy of Israel.

This situation sounds very much like normal Christianity. I have always enjoyed the definition of a Christian that says he is one who is completely fearless, continually cheerful, and constantly in trouble! It is often God's way to let us face troublesome difficulties. But He also has unknown provisions waiting for us, as we will see in Nehemiah.

I shall never forget once sitting at lunch with Cameron Townsend, the founder of Wycliffe Bible Translators, and hearing from his own lips the story of how Wycliffe came into Mexico. This was back in the 1920's at a time when Mexico was very sensitive to anything religious. They had just thrown off the shackles of the [Roman Catholic] church, and they were very opposed to public preaching or the building up of churches. Cameron Townsend went to a tiny Indian village up in the mountains and began to work there, translating the scriptures into their language. Although he could do no preaching, he found that he could help the people. Their economy was suffering because they had poor crops, and he taught them how to dam up a stream and divert the water to their fields. This greatly increased the amount of crops they raised and soon their economy was at a higher level. He also taught them certain industries they could establish right there in the village. Soon word of the changes there got back to Lazaro Cardenas who had just been elected president of Mexico. He had a great heart of concern to help the Indians. One day the President drove out in his limousine to the Indian village, and, when Cameron Townsend saw the presidential limousine, he went up to it to greet the President and introduce himself. The president said, "You're the very man I came to see." He invited Townsend to come to the capital and they became close friends for the duration of Cardenas' presidency. He opened a wide door to the entire work of Wycliffe Translators, and later presidents continued that support. Thus, in a most unexpected way, Wycliffe found an open door for widespread labors through that incident.

In many wonderful ways God demonstrates that He can work in our lives! This is what Nehemiah relied upon. If you are struggling with some habit, some attitude of mind or heart that has possessed you, limited you, and made you difficult to live with, and you want to be free from it, you can expect God to help, often in ways that you cannot anticipate. That is the lesson of this great story.

Honestly Face Reality

Having seized the critical moment and entered the open door that God set before him, Nehemiah now takes the third step to recovery: He honestly faces the full reality of his problem. First, we are told that he enjoyed a brief period of recovery.

I went to Jerusalem, and after staying there three days I set out during the night with a few men.
(Nehemiah 2:11-12a)

He takes time to recover from his journey (his jet lag), and then begins to examine, individually and personally, the extent of the problem he faces.

I had not told anyone what my God had put in my heart to do for Jerusalem. There were no mounts with me except the one I was riding on. By night I went out through the Valley Gate toward the Jackal Well and the Dung Gate, examining the walls of Jerusalem, which had been broken down, and its gates, which had been destroyed by fire. Then I moved on toward the Fountain Gate and the King's Pool [the pool of Siloam], but there was not enough room for my mount to get through; so I went up the valley by night, examining the wall. Finally, I turned back and reentered through the Valley Gate. The officials did not know where I had gone or what I was doing, because as yet I had said nothing to the Jews or the priests or nobles or officials or any others who would be doing the work. (Nehemiah 2:12b-16)

Anticipating opposition, Nehemiah kept his own counsel. He did not tell anybody what he was going to do until he had seen for himself what needed to be done. Apparently the walls were in such a state of ruin that rubble and debris had strewn the valley floor so that he could not even ride his mount through it. He found during this moonlight ride that the walls were in a very sad state of repair.

It is most important that we do something like this in recovering our own ruined areas: We must face the facts as they are, name them, and acknowledge to ourselves and others that they are true. We must not try to cover them over or in any way excuse them.

So Nehemiah personally explores the extent of his problem, and then informs the ones who must do the work with him. This is a moment of challenge when Nehemiah begins to involve others in this work.

Then I said to them, "You see the trouble we are in: Jerusalem lies in ruins, and its gates have been burned with fire. Come, let us rebuild the wall of Jerusalem, and we will no longer be in disgrace." I also told them about the gracious

hand of my God upon me and what the king had said to me. They replied, "Let us start rebuilding." So they began this good work. (Nehemiah 2:17-18)

This is a wonderful example of good leadership. He cannot do this work alone. He must involve others. First, he appeals to their pride, "You can see the ruin around you," he points out. Actually the ruins had been there for almost one hundred years. He is saying, in effect, "That is long enough. It is disgraceful that nothing has been done until now. Let us begin to act." He puts it to them plainly that now is the time because, as he suggests, "God is with us." God had already helped them by moving the heart of the king, setting up the possibility of repair. Now was the time to act.

When leadership steps out like that, it is almost certain to find a following. Nehemiah galvanizes the Jews to action. He appeals to their sense of self-respect, and supplies an encouraging motive to begin.

Opposition Makes Us Strong

But, when you actually start recovering your ruin, you will also meet severe resistance, as Nehemiah discovers.

But when Sanballat the Horonite, Tobiah the Ammonite official and Geshem the Arab [here is a third enemy coming in now] heard about it, they mocked and ridiculed us. "What is this you are doing?" they asked. "Are you rebelling against the king?" (Nehemiah 2:19)

Whenever anybody says, "I will arise and build," Satan always replies, "Then I will arise and oppose." You can count on it! It is a necessary part of the process. God allows it for it is good for us to have opposition.

In a football game, regardless of which team wins, one thing is certain: the game would be meaningless if the teams did not have someone to oppose them. Any member of either team could grab the football and run down and place it over the goal line if there was nobody there to oppose. It is the opposition that makes the players dig in and fight through.

That is what God is after in our lives. It is opposition that makes us strong. If we did not have any difficulty we would be moral cream puffs, unable to function in the kingdom of God. So in His wisdom and grace God allows opposition to rise. Notice the way Nehemiah handles this:

I answered them by saying, "The God of heaven will give us success. We his servants will start rebuilding, but as for you, you have no share in Jerusalem or any claim or historic right to it."
(Nehemiah 2:20)

These men stood outside the covenant of promise. One was a pagan, Sanballat the Horonite; one was a renegade son of Lot, an enemy though also a relative of Israel; and one was a total foreigner, a descendant of Ishmael. All three had no claim to the promise of God to inherit the land. That is why Nehemiah took this stand.

The form their opposition took is also prophetic of our struggles. They first "mocked and ridiculed." This is usually the first weapon the enemy employs. You may have felt it when you began to recover from your ruin. Your friends laughed at your desires to change. They may ridicule your religious convictions and resent with scorn your implied criticisms of their conduct.

Also, Nehemiah's enemies began to threaten and slander him with charges of rebellion and disloyalty. If ridicule does not work, then the opposition stiffens and becomes openly unfriendly and threatening. It is the next level of resistance which those who seek to rebuild will encounter.

These are but pictures for us. They picture something very real: the opposition and the resistance that we will experience from Satan himself. What was true of these opposing forces in Nehemiah's case is true also of Satan. He is a usurper. He has no right to possess humankind. He has tricked us. He has bedeviled us and led us astray. He has confused, manipulated and misled us. Yet he has no right to do so. Jesus came to restore God's property to Him and to loose the hold of the devil upon the human race. That is what He does in our lives. So when we face resistance we must see it as allowed of God to strengthen us, but it has no real right to our lives. We do not have to be weak, failing, and unable to function. We are called to be free. That is the glorious note which the epistle to the Galatians states: "it is for freedom that Christ has set us free!" (Galatians 5:1a).

What that means in practice is that we do not need to be bound by habits from the past. No matter how innocently they may have begun, we do not need to be slaves to drugs, sex, alcohol, tobacco, or whatever it may be controlling and limiting us. Remember Paul's great cry, "I will not be brought under the power of any[thing!]" (1 Corinthians 6:12 KJV). Why? Because he was under the power of God. This is what Nehemiah declares here. There is no necessity to be a slave to a hot temper, or a critical, censorious attitude, or a complaining spirit. These areas of ruin in our lives can be set aside because we are trusting in the program of God. We are expecting God to grant us the grace to stand.

That is why, with great determination, Nehemiah clenches his fist and says, "Look, the God of heaven is with us. He will give us success. We, His servants, will start rebuilding. Do what you like. It is not going to stop us. You are usurpers and have no right to this land."

There are three steps of recovery from ruin that we have covered so far: First, a deep concern that leads us to prayer and to sorrow; then, an opportunity to change to which we must make response; and then, the facing of the facts of our situation honestly and squarely.

When we begin these steps, we have well begun the process of change. Let us take them with confidence that God will enable us to rebuild our walls and restore our gates, to His praise and glory and our grateful relief.

Nehemiah Lesson 3   25

Study Questions

Before you begin each day:
   a. Pray and ask God to speak to you through His Holy Spirit.
   b. Do not use other source books for your answers.
   c. Write your answers and the verses you used.
   d. Remember that the challenge questions are for those who have the time or inclination to do them.
   e. Personal questions are to be shared with the class only if you wish to share.
   f. If you desire, insert your name in the assigned verses to make them more personal.

First Day: Read the Commentary on Nehemiah chapter 2.

1. What meaningful or new thought did you find in the notes on Nehemiah 2, or from your teacher's lecture? What personal application did you choose to apply to your life?

2. Look for a verse in the lesson to memorize this week. Write it down, carry it with you, tack it to your bulletin board, on the dashboard of your car, etc. Make a real effort to learn the verse and its "address" (reference of where it is found in the Bible).

Second Day: Read all of Nehemiah 3, concentrating on verses 1 and 5.

1. a. Who and what does this chapter give us a list of?

   b. Who was going to benefit from the building of the wall?

   c. Does the Lord take notice of who isn't willing to work? See Nehemiah 3:5.

2. What is the first gate in the list of repairs? (Nehemiah 3:1)

3. The sheep which were to be sacrificed in the temple were kept near the Sheep Gate. What does John 1:29 say about our Lord Jesus?

4. Personal: Jesus Christ is the sacrifice for our sins. Faith in Him is the starting point of the Christian life. Have you received Jesus Christ as your Savior? (Read John 1:12-13.) If not, why don't you do it now. Write a prayer telling Him that you believe He paid the price for your sins and asking Him to forgive you. Be certain to thank Him for His sacrifice.

5. Read Romans 12:1. Since Jesus paid the sacrifice for our sin, what sacrifice should we offer?

6. Personal: Have you presented yourself, your life to the Lord as a living sacrifice? Take a moment now and give your entire life to Him, truly making Him Lord of your life. Write 2 Corinthians 5:15 inserting your own name.

26   Joy of Living Bible Studies

Third Day: Read all of Nehemiah 3, concentrating on verses 3-6.

1. From Nehemiah 3:3,6 what were the next gates listed to be rebuilt?

2. The Jeshanah Gate means the "Old Gate." According to Jeremiah 6:16 which path (or gate) should we take? If we walk in the "old way," the "ancient paths," what will it do for us?

3. a. Read John 14:6. Who is "the way"?

   b. Read Matthew 11:29. Yoked oxen walked together, side by side. If we take Jesus' yoke upon us and walk with Him what will be the result?

4. Nehemiah 3:3 refers to the Fish Gate. Read Matthew 4:19. What does Jesus say He will make those who follow Him? What do you think Jesus meant by that?

5. How do the following verses tell us we can be fishers of men?

   Romans 10:13-15a

   1 Peter 3:15

6. Personal: Perhaps you willingly support missionaries who share the Gospel message with others, but do you sometimes have difficulty personally sharing why you have the hope that you do? Using a separate piece of paper write a brief account of why you have put your trust in Jesus Christ. If you like, share it with someone who doesn't know Jesus as Savior.

Fourth Day: Read all of Nehemiah 3, concentrating on verses 13-14.

1. What are the next two gates that are repaired?

2. In scripture a valley represents humility and the judgment against conceit in our lives. What does 1 Peter 5:5b say about pride and humility?

3. Read 1 Corinthians 4:7. Why should we be humble and not boast?

Nehemiah Lesson 3   27

4. The Dung Gate is the gate of elimination, the gate where all the rubbish and corrupt things in the city were brought to the garbage dump. What does 2 Corinthians 7:1 say about this in regard to our own lives?

5. Personal: The Lord wants us to use each of these gates in our own lives. He desires us to walk humbly in His ways, acknowledging our weaknesses and confessing and forsaking our sins. Are there areas of known sin (such as pride, etc.) in your life? Read 1 John 1:9. If you are unaware of your sin, ask God to show you if there are any. Write a prayer listing the areas of pride and sin in your life, confess them to God, then thank Him for forgiving you and cleansing you.

Fifth Day: Read all of Nehemiah 3, concentrating on verses 15 and 26.

1. What gates were referred to in these verses?

2. a. Read John 7:38-39. Who is like a fountain with living water flowing from them?

   b. What did Jesus mean by "living water" in verse 39?

3. Read John 14:26. What will the Holy Spirit do for us?

4. What does Ephesians 5:18b tell us to do?

5. The Water Gate is where Ezra read the Law of God to the people (see Nehemiah 8). In scripture, water is a symbol of the Word of God. This gate did not need to be repaired. From the following verses what are some of the things the Word of God does in our life?

   Romans 12:2

   Hebrews 4:12

   1 Peter 1:23

6. What does Colossians 3:16a tell us to do with the Word of God?

7. Personal: Are you filled with the Holy Spirit and allowing the Word of God to dwell in you? If not, yield yourself to God and ask Him to fill you with His Spirit, then commit yourself to memorizing His Word. Write the verse you have selected to learn for this week.

28   Joy of Living Bible Studies

Sixth Day: Read all of Nehemiah 3, concentrating on verses 28-32.

1. What three gates are listed in verses 28-31?

2. a. The Horse is a symbol of battle in scripture. Read Ephesians 6:12-13. Who is our battle with?

   b. What are we to put on so that we may stand our ground in the battle?

3. Read 2 Corinthians 10:3-5. As Christians, do we wage war in the same manner the world does? What power do our weapons have, and what can we accomplish?

4. What encouragement do we receive from 2 Chronicles 20:15b?

5. The East Gate is the gate through which the returning Messiah will enter the city of Jerusalem. How does Titus 2:13 refer to the return of our Lord?

6. The final gate mentioned in Nehemiah 3 is the Inspection Gate. Where does 2 Corinthians 5:10 say all believers will appear?

7. a. Challenge: Believers' sins were judged and dealt with at the cross of Jesus Christ. In 1 Corinthians 3:9-15 we see believers at the Judgement Seat of Christ. What does this passage say believers will receive? (see verse 14)

   b. If a believer's works are not acceptable will he still be saved? See 1 Corinthians 3:15.

   c. Read Revelation 22:12. How will it be determined what reward a person will receive?

8. Personal: Nehemiah 3 begins and ends with the Sheep gate and so must our Christian walk. Our hope rests in Jesus Christ alone who loved us and gave himself for us (see Galatians 1:3-4). He takes care of the past-forgiving our sins and removing condemnation. He takes care of our present-rebuilding the broken areas of our life and giving us victory in life's battles. He takes care of our future-He is coming again in power and glory and we will dwell with Him forever. Write Romans 8:38-39 inserting your own name.

Nehemiah Lesson 4

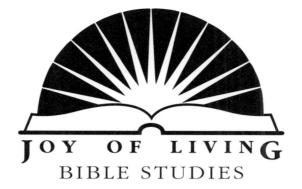

JOY OF LIVING BIBLE STUDIES

Don't Be Paralyzed — Get Organized!

I saw a cartoon recently of two men at a party. Each had a drink in his hand, and they were sitting on the stairway talking while the party was going on. One said to the other, "My view is this: reality is something that you should always treat with respect, but it should not be allowed to control your life." Many people seem to feel that way today. They are fleeing from reality, regarding it as unnecessary. But in the book of Nehemiah we are learning how to return to reality after we have experienced the ruin that comes from following illusion.

Chapter 3 is one of those chapters that appears to consist largely of unpronounceable names and long forgotten people! But it tells the story of the work of repairing the gates and walls of Jerusalem which Nehemiah had been sent there to do. He first aroused the people to the work, and this chapter tells how that work was actually accomplished.

One commentator has said, "God is a great believer in putting names down." That is true. There are many chapters like this in the scriptures. But that should really encourage us. It means that God has not forgotten *our* names either. He may be writing your name down in some great book right now that others will read in times to come.

The central teaching of a chapter like this is that, in putting lives back together, we need and must seek help from each other. We cannot do it alone. This is a great chapter about cooperation. It illustrates the New Testament truth concerning the body of Christ. First Corinthians 12, Romans 12, and other chapters, teach that believers in Christ are part of a worldwide body made up of many members. We belong to each other and so we are to help one another and bear one another's burdens.

We learn from the New Testament that there are two things you cannot say any longer when you become a Christian. The first is, "You do not need me." Everyone in the body of Christ needs everyone else. The second thing is, "I do not need you." You do need others! It is the awareness of that truth that makes a church a living, warm, vital, loving fellowship. I hope you are finding this out more and more.

In a moment we shall look at the importance of keeping in repair the gates of our lives. Gates, in scripture, represent ways of entering into other people's lives and also letting them into ours, of reaching out to others, and allowing them to share our thinking and feeling. As we go through this chapter we shall look in particular at each gate in Jerusalem because each designates a particular quality of the life that we need. The following passage from Second Peter is a very practical example of what I am talking about

For this very reason, make every effort to add to your faith goodness; and to goodness, knowledge; and to knowledge, self-control; and to self-control, perseverance; and to perseverance, godliness; and to godliness, brotherly kindness; and to brotherly kindness, love. (2 Peter 1:5-7)

This exhortation to add certain qualities to our behavior is a marvelous explanation of what it means to repair the gates of our lives. As we do so we will be no longer unfruitful and unproductive. The book of Nehemiah therefore is a picture in Old Testament terms of someone who is restoring the walls and gates of his life.

Before we look at repairing the gates of our lives, I want to skim through this chapter and point out some of the principles for working together that are found in it.

Everyone Should Work

Here is the first one. In summoning the people of Jerusalem to rebuild their walls and their gates we learn from this chapter that all the people were involved. The whole city gave itself over for a period of 52 days to building the walls and the gates. That portrays for us a very important principle of the New Testament: that the ministry of the church in the world today belongs to every believer.

Once, people thought that only the pastor and the hired staff were to do the work of evangelizing, teaching, counseling, healing the hurts of others and serving the needy. Because we have followed that practice far too long, the church is in trouble all over the world. But the ministry belongs to all believers. That is what we see demonstrated in this third chapter. For example look at verses 1-2:

Eliashib the high priest and his fellow priests went to work and rebuilt the Sheep Gate. They dedicated it and set its doors in place, building as far as the Tower of the Hundred, which they dedicated, and as far as the Tower of Hananel. The men of Jericho built the adjoining section, and Zaccur son of Imri built next to them.

(Nehemiah 3:1-2)

Notice that everyone is involved. The priests began the work. That may encourage some who think that preachers never do any work except on Sundays! And with them the Levites worked. A number of rulers are also mentioned. Two men, each of whom ruled half the city of Jerusalem, are getting their hands dirty working on these walls. There were gate keepers, guards, farmers, even perfume makers were involved in the work. I don't know what they did. Their hands probably were pretty soft, but nevertheless they worked on the walls. There were jewelers, pharmacists, merchants and temple servants. Even women were directly involved, as verse 12 points out:

Shallum, son of Hallohesh, ruler of a half-district of Jerusalem, repaired the next section with the help of his daughters. (Nehemiah 3:12)

I wish I had read that to my family years ago when my four daughters were home! They are gone now, so I must rely on someone else's daughters to help me out. Undoubtedly, the wives of these workers did what women always have done through the centuries. They cooked food, served meals, and kept the men at work. But here were women who worked right along with the men. It is encouraging to see this demonstration of equality even in those days.

All Were Volunteers

All of them, by the way, were volunteers. Nobody was conscripted to do this; and no one was paid for their work. Some were residents of Jerusalem and some came from the surrounding cities of Jericho, Tekoa, Mizpah, and other outlying villages of Judea.

So it is also in the body of Christ. We are all engaged in the ministry. I do not know any truth more important for the accomplishing of God's work than that. Yet, in church after church, it is difficult to get people to understand that. You have the great privilege of reaching out in your own neighborhood and doing the work of the ministry there.

Work Together

The second principle that emerges from this chapter is: They worked together. All through this account you will find the phrase "next to him" worked so and so. They took note not only of the workers but also the shirkers. Verse 5 says of the men of Tekoa: "their nobles would not put their shoulders to the work under their supervisors." Did you know that God records goof-offs too? When you will not take up your ministry, God puts your name down in that column as well. But the rest all worked and worked together. Nehemiah had so marvelously organized this that each one had a section of the wall or a gate assigned to him. And some exceeded the work they had been given. Look, for instance, at verse 13:

The Valley Gate was repaired by Hanun and the residents of Zanoah...They also repaired five hundred yards of the wall as far as the Dung Gate.
(Nehemiah 3:13)

Note the *also*. They exceeded their allotment and went on to help somebody else to the extent of repairing 500 yards of wall (an enormous section; probably much of it was still standing and needed little repair).

Work Near Your Home

Then the third principle of cooperation is this: They worked near their home. Look at verse 10: Jedaiah "made repairs opposite his house." Verse 23 tells of certain men who "made repairs in front of their house," and Azariah "made repairs beside his house."

The important truth that emerges is that this is God's design for ministry. God has placed us all strategically where He wants us to be. Your neighborhood, office, or home is where your ministry should be. That is why God put you there. In John 15, Jesus said to His disciples that He had appointed them, and the word means "strategically placed them." He had put them in the place where He wanted them to be. This is brought out beautifully here as we watch these people laboring in their own neighborhood.

Complete Your Task

The fourth principle found here is: Each one completed his assigned task. They kept on until they had finished the work. Some had more to do than others, but no one failed — except the "nobles" of Tekoa who would not dirty their hands.

I have learned through the years that responsibility is always the mark of spiritual maturity. The most mature believers are those who stay with the work that has been assigned to them until it is done.

Each Gate Has Meaning For Us

Now let's look in specific detail at the work they were doing. As we have seen, building a wall and restoring its gates is an illuminating portrayal of a life that is being rebuilt from ruin. You may be hurting right now in some area where you are exposed to peril by some habit you have picked up. You may have a burned gate where evil has access to you. You can be invaded easily and are upset quickly. This account reveals the areas which you need to rebuild if you want to find deliverance and safety.

As we go through this we shall see that each of these gates has a particular meaning which is given to us in the symbol contained in the name of the gate. I know some people have trouble with this kind of an approach. They call it "allegorizing the scriptures," or sometimes, "spiritualizing the text." And they are right, in a sense. There is a danger in working with symbols. It is easy for the imagination to take over and assign arbitrary meanings which have no relation to the text. That has resulted in the past in some very serious abuses of scripture.

Nevertheless, there is a legitimate way to use the symbols of scripture. The Apostle Paul uses allegory and

Nehemiah Lesson 4

also tells us that "all these things happened to [Israel] as types [or symbols] and have been written for our admonition, upon whom the ends of the ages are come," (1 Corinthians 10:11 DBY). If we observe the primary law of scripture, that scripture must interpret itself, we can proceed safely through an account like this. All of these symbols have been consistently used elsewhere in scripture. That is our guideline as we look at this.

Let us go back to the beginning, and look at the gates:

Sheep Gate

The first gate mentioned is the Sheep Gate. This was located where now St. Stephen's Gate, sometimes called the Lion Gate, stands. It is at the northeast corner of the city. Here in Nehemiah's Jerusalem it was called the Sheep Gate, because it was there where the sheep which were to be sacrificed in the temple courts were kept.

It reminds us immediately of Isaiah's great word about Jesus, "as a sheep before her shearers is silent, so he did not open his mouth" (Isaiah 53:7). Remember also that John the Baptist greeted our Lord with the words, "Look, the Lamb of God, who takes away the sin of the world!" (John 1:29). Sheep are a symbol of sacrifice in scripture.

The Sheep Gate is the principle of the cross at work in a Christian's life: It is where you began your life as a Christian. There is to be a principle of death at work in your life — the death of your natural self. The phrase "You are not your own; you were bought at a price" (1 Corinthians 6:19b-20a) expresses that principle beautifully. It is the cross at work. Have you acknowledged that? When you came to Christ you gave up control of your own life. You are no longer to do only what you feel like doing. You are called to obey Him, to follow Him and walk with Him. That means that some of your desires, some of your natural longings, must be put to death. That is the principle of the cross. The Apostle Paul reminds us that we are crucified with Christ unto the world, and the world is crucified unto us (see Galatians 6:14). This is the gate that must be kept in repair if you want to grow into a strong Christian.

Fish Gate

In this counter-clockwise tour around the wall of Jerusalem, the next gate is the Fish Gate. This would be close to where the present Damascus Gate is found. It is called the Fish Gate because fishermen from Galilee and the coast brought their fish into the city through this gate.

Immediately it reminds us of what our Lord said to His disciples: "Follow me, and I will make you fishers of men" (Matthew 4:19 KJV). Throughout the New Testament fishing is a symbol of witnessing to others, of the necessity of acknowledging that you belong to Christ. You witness by your words and actions.

Years ago I asked a High School kid who had been at a summer camp, "How did you get along as a Christian there?" He replied, "Oh, they never found out I was a Christian." That indicated a Fish Gate that needed to be repaired. We are called to be fishers of men.

Old Gate

Then we come to the Jeshanah Gate, which in Hebrew means the "Old Gate." It would be located somewhere near the present Jaffa Gate. This gate represents the old ways of truth versus the new illusions of error. The world is constantly proposing something new, but scripture calls us back to the old way: "Ask for the ancient paths, ask where the good way is, and walk in it" (Jeremiah 6:16).

Somebody has well said, "If something is new, it is not true; and if it is true, then it is not new." That is because truth remains the same throughout the centuries. So this gate calls us back to the basics of life, back to the time-tested paths that have led to stability, security, and order.

What are some of these truths? One that is widely ignored today is that we live in a fallen world; our world is not perfect. It was not intended that it should be after the Fall. We must constantly remind ourselves of that fact and take that into consideration in all relationships. But, nevertheless, we are under a sovereign God, and He can do what He wants. We can come to Him, and believe in Him, and be born again (see John 3:3ff). We can learn the love that disciplines, power that serves, zeal that can wait, hope that endures, and strength that helps others. Those are the old paths. That is what this gate reminds us of.

Valley Gate

In verse 13 we come to the Valley Gate. This would be located at the southwestern corner of Jerusalem. A valley in scripture always represents humility and the judgment of conceit in our lives. John Stott calls humility "that rarest and fairest of Christian virtues." If pride is the ultimate sin, then humility, its opposite, is the ultimate virtue. Peter tells us, "God resists the proud, but gives grace to the humble" (1 Peter 5:5 NKJV).

I often remind myself of that verse when I am tempted to be proud. I remember that feeling and acting in pride means that God will start resisting me. Do you want God working against you? Then go on with your pride. He has ways of resisting that can never be overcome. God resists the proud, yes, but He gives grace and help to the humble! Thus the primary goal of believers is to maintain a sense of humility: We do not have it all together. We are not smart enough to find all the answers ourselves. We do not know how to handle all the difficulties into which we come.

The world applauds pride. It tries to make every individual feel capable of handling anything that comes. It even applauds arrogance. But God applauds humility. Jesus said, "Take my yoke upon you, and learn of me; for I am meek and lowly in heart: and ye shall find rest unto your souls" (Matthew 11:29 KJV). One of the reasons why many people are so restless today is that they have never learned to be humble, to be meek and lowly of heart.

Dung Gate

Then in verse 14 we come to the Dung Gate. That is not a very pleasant name, but it is a necessary activity. It is the gate of elimination, the gate where all the rubbish and corrupt things in the city were brought to the garbage dump in the Hinnom Valley, outside Jerusalem.

It is necessary to have an elimination gate in our lives as well. Paul urges us, "Let us cleanse ourselves from all filthiness of the flesh and spirit" (2 Corinthians 7:1 KJV). One of the reasons many people are unable to function as God wants is because they seldom use the Dung Gate. They do not deal with their secret sin, with private corruption in their own lives. Jesus warned that doing so may be very painful. He said it may be like cutting off an arm or plucking out an eye (see Matthew 5:29). But it is something that has to be done or otherwise it leads to ruin.

Fountain Gate

The sixth gate (verse 15) is the Fountain Gate. This was at the end of the Pool of Siloam, low in the valley in the south. It speaks, of course, of a fountain springing up and reminds us of Jesus' words where He spoke of "streams of living water" (John 7:38) which would come from believers in Him. By that He describes the ministry of the Holy Spirit.

So here is the Spirit-filled life, overflowing to others. As the Apostle Paul said, "Be filled with the Spirit" (Ephesians 5:18). You will notice it comes immediately after the Dung Gate. After the corruption is cleansed away by the consent of the believer, then the cleansing of the Spirit washes clean.

Water Gate

In verse 26 we come to the Water Gate. This is located at the spring of Gihon, where Hezekiah's tunnel begins. In Nehemiah 8 we learn that this is the place where Ezra reads the Law of God to the people.

Water, in scripture, is the symbol of the Word of God. This is the gate that reminds us of our need for the Word of God. The interesting thing about this account is that they did not repair the Water Gate. It did not need repair. The Word of God never needs improvement or repair for it lasts forever. What it needs is to be re-inhabited.

I wonder how many of us need to re-inhabit this gate, and begin again to read and study the Word of God? Jesus said in the Sermon on the Mount, "Man does not live on bread alone." Well, then, what does he live by? "On every word that comes from the mouth of God" (Matthew 4:4). If you want your life filled to the full and enjoying what God intended you to have, it will only be as you come to understand the Word of God.

Horse Gate

Then, reading on, in verse 28 we come to the Horse Gate. This would be found on the eastern wall of Jerusalem. The horse is always the symbol of battle in scripture.

This is the gate that reminds us that we are not on a picnic. We are not on a Caribbean cruise. We are on a battlefield! We are going to be under attack. We are going to be assaulted by surprising events.

There is much joy in the Christian life, but it will not always be without struggle. Everybody is going to face battle. We need to be alert to the fact of spiritual warfare.

East Gate

Then we come to the ninth gate, the East Gate, mentioned in verse 29. Today this is called the Golden Gate. It is on the eastern side, opposite the temple area and facing the rising sun. Thus, it is the gate that speaks of hope and expectation.

This is the gate that is often in ruins in people's lives today. A woman came and told me with tears about a friend of hers who has lost hope. She feels defeated and despairing. She does not want to live any more.

The newspapers recently recorded the tragic story of a mother who lost hope and actually put her two children to death because she saw them having to live in a world that was hopeless. Despair is a common condition with people all around us.

What does the East Gate tell us? It tells us that God has yet a glory awaiting those who trust Him. The story of life does not end in despair and tragedy. Jesus said to His disciples, "When these things begin to take place, stand up and lift up your heads, because your redemption is drawing near" (Luke 21:28). We ought to be like tea kettles — even when they are up to their necks in hot water, they are still singing!

Inspection Gate

Then the last gate is the Inspection Gate, mentioned here in verse 31. The word in Hebrew means "the appointed place." The book of Hebrews tells us, "It is appointed unto men once to die, and after this the judgment" (Hebrews 9:27 KJV) — the inspection! It is a reminder that we must give an account of our journey: We must learn at last the truth about our lives as God sees it.

And yet scripture encourages us by assuring us that it is not a place of condemnation, but rather, as Paul says, "every man will receive his commendation from God" (1 Corinthians 4:5 RSV). It is the place for the giving of rewards, for the acknowledgment of faithful service.

Sheep Gate Stands For The Cross

Then at the end of the chapter we come again to the Sheep Gate, where we began. The Sheep Gate stands for the cross and the cross must be at the beginning and at the end of our lives. Undergirding everything is this principle, *out of death comes life*. Out of the subjection of our natural desires to the will of God comes the life of God filling us full and blessing our hearts.

Isn't this wonderful teaching in this book of Nehemiah? As we compass the walls of Jerusalem, each gate instructs us of the part of our life which needs to be watched, and rebuilt, and repaired. You may find some areas that need repair as you look at your own life today. This is what Nehemiah call us to do: to repair these gates and help ourselves become all that God intended us to be.

Nehemiah Lesson 4

Study Questions

Before you begin each day:
  a. Pray and ask God to speak to you through His Holy Spirit.
  b. Do not use other source books for your answers.
  c. Write your answers and the verses you used.
  d. Remember that the challenge questions are for those who have the time or inclination to do them.
  e. Personal questions are to be shared with the class only if you wish to share.
  f. If you desire, insert your name in the assigned verses to make them more personal.

First Day: Read the Commentary on Nehemiah 3.

1. What meaningful or new thought did you find in the notes on Nehemiah 3, or from your teacher's lecture? What personal application did you choose to apply to your life?

2. Look for a verse in the lesson to memorize this week. Write it down, carry it with you, tack it to your bulletin board, on the dashboard of your car, etc. Make a real effort to learn the verse and its "address" (reference of where it is found in the Bible).

Second Day: Read all of Nehemiah 4, concentrating on verses 1-3.

1. What was Sanballat's response when he heard that the Jews were rebuilding the wall? See Nehemiah 4:1.

2. What remarks did Sanballat make to his associates and the army of Samaria?

3. How did Tobiah the Ammonite respond to Sanballat's remarks?

4. When we choose to follow the Lord and be obedient to Him the enemy of our souls often ridicules and mocks us, sometimes in our own thoughts and sometimes through other people. Read Matthew 27:31, 36-37, 39-41 and write what happened to Jesus as He walked in obedience to the Father.

5. a. Read Hebrews 12:1-3. From verse 2, why did Jesus endure all that happened to Him?

   b. What should you do and what attitude should you have as you deal with the situations life brings your way? See Hebrews 12:1.

   c. Who should we keep our eyes on?

34   Joy of Living Bible Studies

   d. What steps can you take to keep from growing weary and losing heart? See Hebrews 12:3.

6. Personal: Perhaps you have been or are being ridiculed for trusting the Lord or for deciding to follow him. Maybe you've decided to stop practicing a particular sin and those around you don't understand and are ridiculing you (see 1 Peter 4:4). Is your head bowed in shame or embarrassment? Write Psalm 3:3 in your own words.

Third Day: Read all of Nehemiah 4, concentrating on verses 4-5.

1. When Nehemiah heard what the enemy was saying he didn't argue or retaliate. What did he do?

2. Read 1 Peter 2:23. How did Jesus respond to the insults hurled at Him?

3. Nehemiah was named the governor of Judea by king Artaxerxes of Persia. He represented the king's authority in this province. Read Romans 13:1. Who established governmental authority?

4. Read 1 Peter 2:13-14. What are governments to do, according to verse 14?

5. As governor of Judea, how did Nehemiah pray in Nehemiah 4:4-5?

6. a. The insults from the enemy were against Nehemiah as God's appointed ruler, and therefore were against God Himself, and Nehemiah's prayer reflects this view. More than likely the insults that come *your* way are simply against you personally. How does Luke 6:28 say we are to handle those who curse us and despitefully use us?

   b. Personal: Is there someone who has done you wrong? Why not write a prayer right now asking God to bless them, and bring them to repentance and to the knowledge of Jesus Christ as Savior.

Fourth Day: Read all of Nehemiah 4, concentrating on verses 6-23.

1. Although the enemy had mocked and insulted God's people and God's work the people didn't stop working. What did the enemy do next to try to stop God's work? See Nehemiah 4:7-8.

2. What two things did God's people do in response? (See Nehemiah 4:9.)

3. In Nehemiah 4:10-12 we see those who were tired becoming discouraged and fearful. How did Nehemiah handle this problem in verses 13 and 14?

Nehemiah Lesson 4   35

4. What was the result of these actions in Nehemiah 4:15?

5. Describe how the people continued to work in Nehemiah 4:16-23.

6. a. Read 1 Peter 5:7. How are we to deal with our anxieties and why can we do this?

   b. Then what actions are we to take to protect us from our enemy, the Devil? See 1 Peter 5:8.

   c. Personal: Nehemiah was aware of the plots of the enemy. He prayed, took what action he could, trusted the Lord and kept working. Is there something you are fearful or anxious about? Write a prayer giving your fear to the Lord. Ask Him to show you if there is some action you should take.

Fifth Day: Read all of Nehemiah 5, concentrating on verses 1-13.

1. Nehemiah has taken care of the problems from the enemies round about them. Where does a new problem come from? See Nehemiah 5:1.

2. What specific problems are mentioned in Nehemiah 5:2-4?

3. What were some of the Jews having to do because of their debts and taxes? See Nehemiah 5:5.

4. a. From Nehemiah 5:6-9, what was adding to the problem?

   b. Challenge: Using your dictionary look up the meaning of *usury.*

5. What two steps does Nehemiah say they should take to remedy the problem? (See Nehemiah 5:10-11.)

36   Joy of Living Bible Studies

6. What is the response of the nobles in Nehemiah 5:12a?

7. a. Write in your own words what Matthew 5:23-24 says.

   b. Personal: Is there someone you have wronged? What steps can you take to make it right? Ask God to help you follow through with these steps.

Sixth Day: Read all of Nehemiah 5, concentrating on verses 14-19.

1. Was the governor to receive anything from those he governed? See Nehemiah 5:14.

2. How did the governors prior to Nehemiah treat God's people? (Nehemiah 5:15)

3. a. According to Nehemiah 5:14,15,16, and 18, what actions *didn't* Nehemiah take and why?

   b. From Nehemiah 5:16-17, what actions *did* Nehemiah take?

4. What do the following verses say about those who do the Lord's work?
   Matthew 10:10

   1 Corinthians 9:9-11

   Galatians 6:6

   1 Peter 5:2-3

5. What does Galatians 6:10 say we are to do and to whom?

6. Personal: There are many ways of doing good for others: giving of finances, food or clothing; giving of talents and abilities (e.g. cleaning someone's home, baby-sitting for a harried mother, helping with yard work for someone unable to do it themselves); visiting or phoning the sick or shut-in's; praying for people. Can you think of other ways of doing good to others? Is there someone you can help? Make a commitment and carry through with it this week. If you wish, share your ideas and actions with your group.

Nehemiah
Lesson 5

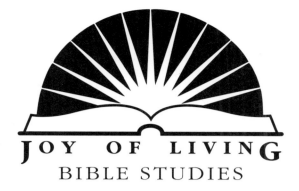

JOY OF LIVING
BIBLE STUDIES

Don't Back Down — Build Up

Most of us have had experience with what is called "Murphy's Law," the idea that if anything can go wrong, it will. For instance, if you try to fix something, Murphy's Law says it will take longer than you anticipated; it will cost more than you expected; it will break down before it is paid for; and someone will not like it when it is done!

We have come to such a circumstance in chapter 4 of the book of Nehemiah. Here, Nehemiah faces severe and violent opposition to his work of rebuilding the walls and gates of Jerusalem. We have seen that this rebuilding and reconstruction pictures for us the steps to recovery from areas of damage or ruin in our own lives. As we have been following Nehemiah in this great project we first saw his heartfelt concern and anguish over the damaged walls and ruined gates of the capital city of his country. It echoes the concern and the anguish that many of us may feel about areas that have been damaged in our lives by sinful habits, wrong attitudes, or feelings of bitterness or resentment. Then we have seen Nehemiah's quick response to the opportunity to rebuild when it was given to him. This reflects our need to respond to opportunities that may be given to us to recover. We have observed Nehemiah's honest facing of the magnitude of his task when he got to Jerusalem. He made a careful survey of the walls and the gates to see how much he had to repair. We then noted his first meeting with the enemies who would later oppose him, and, finally, we observed his care in organizing and sharing the labor of this great project as it got under way.

Now, in chapter 4, the opposition takes off its gloves, and the real battle begins. We, like Nehemiah, have an enemy who opposes us with craftiness and power. Against every effort on our part to get our lives together and recover from damage, hurt, and ruin, we will experience opposition from the enemy.

Opposition by Ridicule

Almost invariably the enemy's first attempt to halt such recovery is to discourage us through ridicule, derision or rejection. So Nehemiah discovers here.

When Sanballat heard that we were rebuilding the wall, he became angry and was greatly incensed. He ridiculed the Jews, and in the presence of his associates and the army of Samaria, he said, "What are those feeble Jews doing? Will they restore their wall? Will they offer sacrifices? Will they finish in a day? Can they bring the stones back to life from those heaps of rubble — burned as they are?"

Tobiah the Ammonite, who was at his side, said, "What they are building — if even a fox climbed up on it, he would break down their wall of stones." (Nehemiah 4:1-3)

Hear the scorn, derision and sarcasm in those comments! Many of us, perhaps, have experienced this kind of attack. I know personally of people who are unwilling to do what is right because they fear their friends will laugh at them or mock them. I know a man who is unable to stop drinking because his drinking friends make fun of him. Yet drink is destroying his life. I know of others who are hooked on drugs, but they do not want to stop because they are afraid they will be laughed at.

Perhaps you have had someone say to you when you are trying to stop something that was wrong, "Who do you think you are anyhow? Do you think you are better than us?" Or perhaps someone says, "You've made a good start but you won't hold out. You won't last."

Pray, Don't Retaliate

Nehemiah persists against the mockery and scorn of his enemies. Notice particularly what his response was to this attack. As you might expect, it is one of prayer:

Hear us, O our God, for we are despised. Turn their insults back on their own heads. Give them over as plunder in a land of captivity. Do not cover up their guilt or blot out their sins from your sight, for they have thrown insults in the face of the builders. (Nehemiah 4:4-5)

Nehemiah regards this attack as an insult against God Himself. Note that he does not argue back, nor does he retaliate. He does not blister these men with angry rebuttal. He simply responds by praying. It reminds us of Peter's words about Jesus: "When they hurled their insults at him, he did not retaliate, when he suffered, he made no threats" (1 Peter 2:23). This is a helpful picture of how to handle that kind of attack.

"Well," you say, "this is a very strange prayer. Nehemiah is asking that these people be destroyed. What happened to forgiveness and love?" It is true that Jesus taught us to bless those who persecute us, to pray for our enemies and those who despitefully use us, and to do good to them. So how do we square Nehemiah's prayer with what our Lord taught? The answer, of course, is to remember who it is that is praying. This is not Nehemiah, the ordinary citizen, the individual, who has been injured by someone's personal attack. This is the Governor of Judea, praying about maintaining order and peace in his land and forwarding the work that God Himself had sent him to do. This is a different kind of prayer because it is a prayer of an authority seeking to handle the problem of evil.

Some years ago a madman opened fire on helpless children in a school playground, killing a number of them. The killer took his own life, but if he had escaped, what would you think of the authorities if they treated him with forgiveness? The first task of government is not mercy, but justice! Mercy is appropriate when it is an individual matter, but justice must prevail in government.

So, having prayed, Nehemiah returns to the work. "So we rebuilt the wall till all of it reached half its height, for the people worked with all their heart" (Nehemiah 4:6). Ridicule and sarcasm did not destroy their confidence. They unhesitatingly went ahead with the work. But the enemies of God are not through. They grow even angrier, and resolve upon the use of force.

But when Sanballat, Tobiah, the Arabs, the Ammonites and the men of Ashdod heard that the repairs to Jerusalem's walls had gone ahead and that the gaps were being closed, they were very angry. They all plotted together to come and fight against Jerusalem and stir up trouble against it.
(Nehemiah 4:7-8)

The enemy mobilizes its forces, escalating the attack, and begins to plan direct violence. When you begin to move with God to change things in your life for the better you will find that you are met first with derision and if you keep persisting, someone is going to get very upset with you and attack you in a vicious, perhaps physical way.

But see how Nehemiah reacts. He still relies on prayer. "But we prayed to our God and posted a guard day and night to meet this threat" (Nehemiah 4:9). He does more than pray, however. He posts a guard as well. Prayer and preparedness! This blending of the resources of the spiritual life with those of the material world is a marvelous picture of how believers ought to face threats, recognizing that we need action on both levels.

Opposition by Propaganda

Still the enemy persists and now he launches a propaganda campaign: "Meanwhile, the people in Judah said, 'The strength of the laborers is giving out, and there is so much rubble that we cannot rebuild the wall'" (Nehemiah 4:10). This is understandable. There was an enormous amount of debris and broken stones which had to be cleared away before they could get to the walls. It must have been very discouraging. These people were at the point of exhaustion and frustration.

The enemy immediately takes advantage of that weakness and discouragement:

Also our enemies said, "Before they know it or see us, we will be right there among them and will kill them and put an end to the work." Then the Jews who lived near them came and told us ten times over [that is a sign they are very agitated by this], **"Wherever you turn, they will attack us."**
(Nehemiah 4:11-12)

Have you faced something like that? Were you ever threatened at work when you tried to correct an immoral or illegal practice? Perhaps someone said to you, "Keep that up and you may lose your job here." You may have been threatened with demotion, or with eviction from your apartment. You may even have been invited out in the parking lot to face a physical attack. These kind of things are quite possible when, like Nehemiah, we begin to right wrongs.

Nehemiah's Response

Nehemiah's response is very deliberate, enlightening, and helpful. First, he carefully looks over the situation.

Therefore I stationed some of the people behind the lowest points of the wall at the exposed places, posting them by families, with their swords, spears and bows. After I looked things over...
(Nehemiah 4:13-14a)

He carefully assesses the situation and evaluates what is needed. This approach is necessary if we are going to improve our own lives. We must observe exactly where we are under attack. What are we addicted to? A wrong habit, a drug, an attitude of mind? Bitterness of spirit? When we have identified the source of attack, we must post a guard at that point. This is what Nehemiah does. He assesses the situation and prepares for a full assault.

Then, second, Nehemiah reviews the spiritual resources available to them.

After I looked things over, I stood up and said to the nobles, the officials and the rest of the people, "Don't be afraid of them. Remember the Lord, who is great and awesome, and fight for your brothers, your sons and your daughters, your wives and your homes." When our enemies heard that we were aware of their plot and that God had frustrated it, we all returned to the wall, each to his own work. (Nehemiah 4:14-15)

Because they were believers they had a power at work in their lives that their enemies knew nothing about. They had invisible resources they could count on in times of danger. The great and awesome God who was with them would stand with them in their peril. When they remembered this, they became reassured and renewed in courage. The enemy saw that they could achieve nothing with their attacks. God had frustrated their plottings by Nehemiah's simple reminder that God was with His people and would fight for them.

One of my favorite passages of the New Testament is found in Paul's second letter to Timothy. Paul is a prisoner in Rome, and Timothy, a rather timid young man, is all alone and feeling discouraged in the great pagan city of Ephesus. The great apostle writes to him this word of advice: "Remember Jesus Christ, raised from the dead" (2 Timothy 2:8). Timothy was not alone. God was with him. Jesus is risen! He is awesome. He is strong. He is powerful. Reckon upon Him and you will be able to stand against the most subtle temptation and the most dangerous threats that come against you. Nehemiah goes on in the next passage to maintain his readiness.

From that day on, half of my men did the work, while the other half were equipped with spears, shields, bows and armor. The officers posted themselves behind all the people of Judah who were building the wall. Those who carried materials did their work with one hand and held a weapon in the other, and each of the builders wore his sword at his side as he worked. But the man who sounded the trumpet stayed with me. (Nehemiah 4:16-18)

He now combines the work with the war. Each man goes to work with an instrument in one hand for labor and a sword in the other for battle. Thus, he is ready for either. Charles Spurgeon, the great English preacher of the nineteenth century, published a newspaper in his church, called: *The Sword and the Trowel.* The name was clearly derived from Nehemiah. Spurgeon said that Christians should always be building the kingdom of God, but be ready for battle at any time.

Verse 21 through the end of the chapter shows the degree of self-sacrifice involved:

So we continued the work with half the men holding spears, from the first light of dawn till the stars came out. At that time I also said to the people, "Have every man and his helper stay inside Jerusalem at night, so they can serve us as guards by night and workmen by day." Neither I, nor my brothers nor my men nor the guards with me took off our clothes; each had his weapon, even when he went for water. (Nehemiah 4:21-23)

There is an alertness, a vigilance here, that does not even allow for comfort. To put this in New Testament terms, they are ready to endure hardship for the sake of the Lord. It must have been very uncomfortable, sleeping in their clothes on the hard ground beside the walls, but they were ready for anything the cause demanded.

Trouble From Within

The Unseen Enemy tries yet another approach. Nehemiah has successfully handled the threatened attack from without, but now he runs into a problem from within his own ranks. "Now the men and their wives raised a great outcry against their Jewish brothers" (Nehemiah 5:1).

Here is internal strife, no longer attack from without but trouble from within. You may experience that too, in your struggle to recover some area of your life. You may run into family problems, pressures, and problems with those who work with you, perhaps even from other brothers and sisters in the Lord. In this case it was a clash between the workers and the officials, the laborers and the overseers who were working on this project.

While they were working on the walls day and night they had no time to plant crops and yet they had to eat. Verse 3 reveals what made it difficult: "We are mortgaging our fields, our vineyards and our homes to get grain during the famine" (Nehemiah 5:3). Does this sound like some of you? You have had to mortgage your property to make a living or to remain in this area. Perhaps you have been forced to borrow money to keep your family or yourself alive. This was the complaint of some to Nehemiah. And,

Still others were saying, "We have had to borrow money to pay the king's tax on our fields and vineyards. Although we are of the same flesh and blood as our countrymen and though our sons are as good as theirs, yet we have to subject our sons and daughters to slavery." (Nehemiah 5:4-5a)

In those times if you could not pay your taxes or debts, you sold your children or your wife to be slaves in order to pay what you owed.

To a great degree these were justified complaints. Nehemiah deals with them earnestly and forthrightly. He could not change the conditions, but now he reveals the real problem.

When I heard their outcry and these charges, I was very angry. I ... accused the nobles and officials. I told them, "You are exacting usury from your own countrymen! ... As far as possible, we have bought back our Jewish brothers who were sold to the Gentiles. Now you are selling your brothers, only for them to be sold back to us!" They kept quiet, because they could find nothing to say. (Nehemiah 5:6-8)

Usury, of course, is charging interest for money which has been loaned — a common practice in our day. Moses had spoken directly to this issue. He said that when a Jew lent money to another Jew he was not to charge any interest. Verse 11 tells what the interest rate was. It was one hundredth part per month, which would be 1% or a total of 12% per year. This does not sound excessive to us, but it was enough to outrage Nehemiah.

What you are doing is not right. Shouldn't you walk in the fear of our God to avoid the reproach of our Gentile enemies? ... But let the exacting of usury stop! Give back to them immediately their fields, vineyards, olive groves and houses, and

also the usury you are charging them — the hundredth part of the money, grain, new wine and oil. (Nehemiah 5:9b-11)

This was more than a demand to end the practice of usury. He was insisting on restitution as well. They must give back their unjust gains. And their reaction was surprising. "'We will give it back,' they said. 'And we will not demand anything more from them. We will do as you say'" (Nehemiah 5:12a). They were stricken by conscience because they knew from the scriptures that what they were doing was wrong.

This suggests that believers ought to be very careful about taking advantage of others, especially other Christians, and getting rich at their expense. Scripture condemns this practice as uncaring and heedless of the poor testimony it presents to others.

Nehemiah is encouraged by their promise that they will not do this. But he does not stop with that:

Then I summoned the priests and made the nobles and officials take an oath to do what they had promised. ... At this the whole assembly said, "Amen," and praised the LORD. And the people did as they had promised. (Nehemiah 5:12b-13b)

Final Action

The rest of the chapter details the final action of Nehemiah to overcome this internal strife. He has first uncovered the real cause. He shows that it is simple greed that is the problem. He confronts the overseers with it, rebuking them and showing them it is wrong. He gains their promise, always by God's help, to stop this practice. There is a place and time for forthright, blunt confrontation in our relationships with others. Sometimes we need to point out to people that what they are doing is wrong and help them to see what needs to be done. That is what Nehemiah does. Then he does one final thing.

Moreover, from the twentieth year of King Artaxerxes, when I was appointed to be their governor in the land of Judah, until his thirty-second year — twelve years — neither I nor my brothers ate the food allotted to the governor. But the earlier governors — those preceding me — placed a heavy burden on the people and took forty shekels of silver from them in addition to food and wine. Their assistants also lorded it over the people. (Nehemiah 5:14-15a)

This is the familiar picture of officials who get rich by using their power over people. They enhance their own lavish life-styles and treat others with disdain and scorn. Nehemiah says, "I did not do that." But his motivation is noteworthy.

But out of reverence for God I did not act like that. Instead, I devoted myself to the work on this wall.

All my men were assembled there for the work; we did not acquire any land. (Nehemiah 5:15b-16)

He was not acting simply to win favor among the people or to gain reelection to the job. It was not even to correct previous extortion. It was because he loved God! Because he was grateful for what God had done for him, he passed it on to others. Jesus said, "Freely you have received, freely give" (Matthew 10:8). This sense of gratitude is the most powerful motivation Christians can experience.

Furthermore, a hundred and fifty Jews and officials ate at my table, as well as those who came to us from the surrounding nations. Each day one ox, six choice sheep and some poultry were prepared for me, and every ten days an abundant supply of wine of all kinds. (Nehemiah 5:17-18a)

All this was at his own expense. He had every right to this as the governor, but he did not take it. He paid for it himself, for he says:

In spite of all this, I never demanded the food allotted to the governor, because the demands were heavy on these people. (Nehemiah 5:18b)

What a remarkable picture of compassion and concern for those who had much less! Nehemiah was willing to sacrifice himself in order to help them, and even to allow them to eat at his table the food that he paid for himself.

So this great man of prayer closes with a very brief prayer. "Remember me with favor, O my God, for all I have done for these people" (Nehemiah 5:19). Does that sound self-serving and as though he is bargaining with God? Some read it that way, but that is to read it wrongly. What Nehemiah is doing is recognizing God's gracious promise that He will care for the needs of those who walk with Him. He will help them, but not always economically or materially. It may be spiritual blessing that will enrich them more than material gain. In the midst of extreme poverty, this has often been the case. But God will always bless, for in chapter 6 of Hebrews the writer says, "God is not unjust; he will not forget your work and the love you have shown him as you have helped his people and continue to help them" (Hebrews 6:10). You can count on that. What Nehemiah is really praying is, "Lord, I sought to do your will, now respond according to your gracious nature." He does not demand anything nor does he ask for anything specifically. He does not bargain with God. He is merely calling upon God to honor His promise.

There are two major lessons that loom forth from these chapters: First, when we face enmity, we should do so with careful preparation, perseverance, and above all, prayer. But, when we face discord and internal strife, let us do so with justice, with honest confrontation, and by setting a good example ourselves. As we do this, God will enable us to solve the problems that face us and move toward rebuilding the ruined areas of our lives.

Nehemiah Lesson 5   41

Study Questions

Before you begin each day:
   a. Pray and ask God to speak to you through His Holy Spirit.
   b. Do not use other source books for your answers.
   c. Write your answers and the verses you used.
   d. Remember that the challenge questions are for those who have the time or inclination to do them.
   e. Personal questions are to be shared with the class only if you wish to share.
   f. If you desire, insert your name in the assigned verses to make them more personal.

First Day: Read the Commentary on Nehemiah 4-5.

1. What meaningful or new thought did you find in the notes on Nehemiah 4-5, or from your teacher's lecture? What personal application did you choose to apply to your life?

2. Look for a verse in the lesson to memorize this week. Write it down, carry it with you, tack it to your bulletin board, on the dashboard of your car, etc. Make a real effort to learn the verse and its "address" (reference of where it is found in the Bible).

Second Day: Read all of Nehemiah 6, concentrating on verses 1-4.

1. When Sanballat, Tobiah, and Geshem saw that their previous plots had failed how did they attempt to stop Nehemiah? (Nehemiah 6:2)

2. a. Nehemiah ran into opposition the moment he set his heart to obey God's command to rebuild the walls and gates of Jerusalem. Where does our opposition come from, according to Ephesians 6:12?

   b. It is important that we be aware of Satan's schemes so that he will not outwit us (see 2 Corinthians 2:11). We have seen how he can be like a "roaring lion" seeking someone to devour (see 1 Peter 5:8). Read 2 Corinthians 11:14b. What is another way the enemy comes against us?

3. In Nehemiah 6:3 what was Nehemiah's response to the enemy?

4. Did the enemy give up when Nehemiah refused to be tricked by them? See Nehemiah 6:4.

5. a. Read 2 Timothy 3:12-15. We know that if we follow the Lord we will suffer persecution from the enemy. What does verse 13 say will happen to evil men and those pretending to be godly?

   b. What are we to do? See 2 Timothy 3:14-15.

6. Personal: Nehemiah refused to be swayed from the work of God by either fear and threats, or compromise and friendship with the enemy. Are you facing or have you ever faced either of these situations? How did you handle it? Write 2 Timothy 3:14 again, including your name to personalize it.

Third Day: Read all of Nehemiah 6, concentrating on verses 5-9.

1. When offers of 'friendship' failed to compromise Nehemiah what does the enemy resort to?

2. Were the things in the letter true? How did Nehemiah handle this attack? See Nehemiah 6:8.

3. Challenge: What do you think might have happened if this letter were sent to the king and he believed it?

4. a. What did the enemy hope to accomplish with the lie? See Nehemiah 6:9a.

   b. How did Nehemiah handle this problem? (Nehemiah 6:9b)

5. a. Read Psalm 37:5-11. From verse 6, what will the Lord do for those who commit their way to Him and trust in Him?

   b. What should be our attitude when wicked men seem to succeed in the evil they plot? (Psalm 37:7)

   c. Why should we refrain from worrying and being angry? (Psalm 37:8)

   d. From Psalm 37:9 and 11, what will be the difference between the wicked and those who trust in the Lord?

   e. Will this happen immediately? (Psalms 37:10)

6. Personal: Have you ever had someone lie or bear false witness against you? How did you feel? Has the truth come out yet? Read Psalm 42:11, and write it in your own words.

Fourth Day: Read all of Nehemiah 6, concentrating on verses 10-14.

1. The enemy just doesn't give up on Nehemiah; instead they change tactics. What does the prophet tell Nehemiah he should do and why? See Nehemiah 6:10.

2. Read Numbers 3:10 and 18:6-7. Only the priests were to approach the sanctuary. What was to happen to anyone who did not obey this?

Nehemiah Lesson 5

3. Read Isaiah 8:16-20. Would God have a prophet give a prophecy that contradicts what He has said in His Word? Write verse 20 here.

4. What did Nehemiah realize in Nehemiah 6:12-13?

5. How did Nehemiah handle this problem? (verses 11 & 14).

6. Personal: Have you ever been tempted to handle a problem in a manner that contradicts what God has said in His Word? Do you think God will bless actions that contradict what He has said in His Word? Look up the word *blessed* in the dictionary, then write James 1:25 in your own words. Ask God to help you be obedient to His Word.

Fifth Day: Read all of Nehemiah 6, concentrating on verses 15-19.

1. Even with all the opposition the wall was completed. How long had it taken them? (Nehemiah 6:15)

2. What was the response of those who had opposed the building of the wall? (Nehemiah 6:16a)

3. Why did they lose their self-confidence? (Nehemiah 6:16b)

4. a. Challenge: In each of the following verses how do the heathen nations respond to what God has done?

   Exodus 14:25

   Numbers 23:23

   Joshua 5:1

   Psalm 126:2

44   Joy of Living Bible Studies

b. Do you think God was glorified on each of these occasions?

5. Personal: Are you sometimes discouraged because things don't happen as quickly as you would like? Do you sometimes get tired of the oppression and opposition of the enemy? Read Romans 8:25-31. Do you find encouragement from these verses? Who always interceeds for the Christian? Write Romans 8:31 inserting your own name.

Sixth Day: Read all of Nehemiah 7.

1. Why did Nehemiah give his brother Hananiah charge over Jerusalem? (Nehemiah 7:2)

2. a. Even after the walls were built did the people let down their guard? (Nehemiah 7:3)

   b. Should we ever let down our guard? Read 1 Thessalonians 5:6.

3. What did Nehemiah do next? See Nehemiah 7:5.

4. Read Nehemiah 7:63-65. Why were the descendants of Hobaiah, Hakkoz and Barzilla excluded from the priesthood and not allowed to eat any of the sacred food?

5. a. Only those who were truly Israelites could live in Jerusalem and only those who descended from Aaron could be amongst the priesthood; this was their right, their inheritance. Read 1 Peter 1:3-4. What type of inheritance has God promised to those who are born again as His children?

   b. Personal: What about you? Have you been born again as God's child? (Read John 1:12 and 3:3.) If not, why don't you pray right now, asking God to forgive your sins and accepting His son Jesus Christ as your Savior. Write 1 Peter 1:3-4 again, inserting your own name.

Nehemiah
Lesson 6

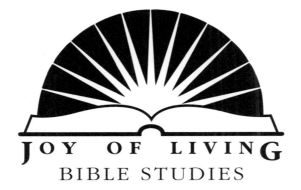

JOY OF LIVING BIBLE STUDIES

Don't Vacillate — Perpetuate!

One thing that clearly emerges from the book of Nehemiah is that life is a battle from beginning to end. Nehemiah ran into opposition the moment he set his heart to obey God's command to rebuild the walls and gates of Jerusalem. He faced difficulty before he even got to the city. Then, after he reached Jerusalem, enemies rose up to oppose everything he did. You may not yet have experienced all that in your Christian life, but you will!

In Ephesians 6:12 the Apostle Paul warns, "Our struggle is not against flesh and blood." Men and women, other humans, are not really our problem. What we are up against is invisible forces: "the powers of this dark world" (Ephesians 6:12b), Paul calls them. Thus we are confronted by an invisible enemy who hates law and order, and justice and peace. He loves to mangle, trap, destroy and murder. He lives to oppose the work of God in creating harmony, beauty, love and respect. That is what we are battling.

How the Devil Operates

Here in Nehemiah, as in many other places in scripture, we learn that the devil has two main ways of working. First, the devil comes, as Peter says, "as a roaring lion, ... seeking whom he may devour" (1 Peter 5:8b KJV). A lion is a very dangerous, powerful and fearsome animal. He is so strong that one bite from his jaws can crush the thickest bone in the human body, the thigh bone. One blow from his mighty paw can smash a human skull like an egg shell. This strength portrays the devil's ability to strike at us with calamity, disaster and frightening circumstances that chill our blood. That is one way the enemy works in our lives.

But he has another capacity also. The Bible reveals that he can suddenly become what the scripture calls "an angel of light" (2 Corinthians 11:14b). He comes with smiling, gracious accommodation, enticing promises and flattering words, assuring us that what he proposes will cost us nothing.

But either route, fear or flattery, will result in destruction for us. Ruin will begin. We must be on our guard against each of these approaches. That is why Paul says of himself, "We are not ignorant of [the devil's] devices" (2 Corinthians 2:11 KJV). Nehemiah likewise teaches us to be aware of how the devil goes about his work.

New Tactics

In Nehemiah 6, following a series of attacks and threats against him in an effort to intimidate him, the enemies of Nehemiah suddenly change their tactics. Suddenly they resort to friendliness and persuasion.

When word came to Sanballat, Tobiah, Geshem the Arab and the rest of our enemies that I had rebuilt the wall and not a gap was left in it — though up to that time I had not set the doors in the gates — Sanballat and Geshem sent me this message: "Come, let us meet together in one of the villages on the plain of Ono."

But they were scheming to harm me; so I sent messengers to them with this reply: "I am carrying on a great project and cannot go down. Why should the work stop while I leave it and go down to you?" Four times they sent me the same message, and each time I gave them the same answer. (Nehemiah 6:1-4)

They could not stop the work of building by threat and attack, so they switched their tactics. You will experience this too when you try to correct wrong things in your life. It is possible that your friends will become your most dangerous foes. Many people today are faltering in their Christian pilgrimage because they listen to the advice of their friends. But those friends may not be reflecting the wisdom of God. They may be picking up the attitudes and wisdom of the world around. It sounds like good advice because so many people follow it, but it may be totally wrong. We must check everything by the word and wisdom of the scriptures.

These erstwhile enemies suddenly become Nehemiah's friends and invite him to a conference down on the plain of Ono. Some commentators suggest that they were trying to trick him into leaving Jerusalem, where he had armed support, to come to a conference where they could set upon him and perhaps kill him. Nehemiah evidently senses this. He firmly declines, saying, "I am carrying on a great project, and I cannot go down. Why should the work stop while I leave it and go down to you?"

That is a great answer. We need especially to note the reasons he gives. On the surface it seems a surly response to their invitation to meet together. But Nehemiah sees through their scheme and refuses to go along, even though they pressure him four different times.

You, too, may experience continuing pressure to change your mind and go along with something that is wrong. Many have fallen after a proper refusal, simply because they gave in to repeated pressure. But Nehemiah persists in his refusal. Here is his reason: "I am doing a great work," he says. "I have a great calling. God has committed a tremendous project to me, and if I leave, it will be threatened."

Resist Temptation

One of the most helpful things that we can do to resist temptation is to remember that God has called us to a great task. This is true of every believer in Christ. I do not care how young or how old you are in the Lord, you are called to a tremendous work today. That task is: to model a different life-style so that those who are being ruined by wrongful practices will see something that offers them hope and deliverance. If they see in you peace in the midst of confusion, an invisible support that keeps you steady and firm under pressure, they will learn that there is another way to live than the destructive way they have chosen. That is the great work that God has called us to. We ought never to give allegiance to anything less.

I read years ago of a missionary in China, a very capable young man who did a great job as a linguist and a diplomat in his work for the Lord. His abilities were so outstanding that one of the American companies in China tried to hire him. They offered him an attractive job with a salary to match, but he turned them down. He told them that God had sent him to China as a missionary and that was what he was going to do. He thought that would end the matter, but instead they came back with a better offer and an increase in salary. He turned that down too, but again they came back, doubling the salary that had originally been proposed. Finally he said to them, "It is not your salary that is too little. It's the job that's too small!"

This is essentially what Nehemiah is saying here. He has a great work, and he is not going to forsake it for anything less. He is confronted with an offer that seems to promise peace and support, and yet is filled with danger which he successfully avoids by refusing to leave his calling.

Threats Again

When the enemy cannot accomplish his purpose by offering peace and friendliness, he switches back to his original tactic of threats and danger.

Then, the fifth time, Sanballat sent his aide to me with the same message, and in his hand was an unsealed letter in which was written: "It is reported among the nations — and Geshem [the Arab] says it is true — that you and the Jews are plotting to revolt, and therefore you are building the wall. Moreover, according to these reports you are about to become their king and have even

appointed prophets to make this proclamation about you in Jerusalem: 'There is a king in Judah!' Now this report will get back to the king; so come, let us confer together. (Nehemiah 6:5-7)

This arm-twisting tactic is designed to put pressure on Nehemiah to yield to their solicitation, and thus fall into their trap. But he resists because he sees it for what it really is, an enticement based upon lies and without basis in any fact whatsoever. Note that it was an "unsealed letter." In other words, it was designed for everybody involved in delivering it to read, and thus spread around the lie that Nehemiah was trying to make himself king. Notice how he responds.

I sent him this reply: "Nothing like what you are saying is happening; you are just making it up out of your head." (Nehemiah 6:8)

That is the way to respond to such a charge — just a flat denial. There is no attempt to disprove their accusation. He merely states, "That is a lie. There is no truth in it." And then, invariably, his response is one of prayer.

They were all trying to frighten us, thinking, "Their hands will get too weak for the work, and it will not be completed." But I prayed, "Now strengthen my hands." (Nehemiah 6:9)

Their tactics were to get the people to think that Nehemiah had some hidden motive — his own glory — for rebuilding the wall, hoping that the workers would thus become discouraged and quit. Nehemiah simply prays, "Lord, do not let that happen. Strengthen me to work all the harder." This great response will help us if we are charged with some kind of slanderous lie like this.

More Subterfuge

Once again the enemy switches his tactics. He reverts again to subterfuge:

One day I went to the house of Shemaiah son of Delaiah, the son of Mehetabel, who was shut in at his home. He said, "Let us meet in the house of God, inside the temple, and let us close the temple doors, because men are coming to kill you — by night they are coming to kill you." (Nehemiah 6:10)

This word comes in the form of a prophecy, but this man is a false prophet. He claims to have hidden, perhaps occult, knowledge. That is suggested here by this word that he was "shut in" at his home. That does not mean that he was sick; it rather suggests that for some religious reason he was secluding himself. This is frequently the case with those who claim to be seers and in touch with the invisible world. They sit behind curtains in semidarkness, trying to create a sense of mystery, as though they know more about inscrutable things than others.

What he says sounds logical. "Some people are out to get you. They are going to kill you," he charges. Nehemiah certainly believes that! The man suggests, "Come on up here and we will go into the temple and shut the

Nehemiah Lesson 6

doors. They will not dare attack you there." That sounds good, but immediately Nehemiah detects something wrong. He knows that he is not permitted to go into the temple, for only priests could enter the temple, and he was a layman. There is nothing wrong with being a layman, but it was simply not right for him to do this. So he answers:

But I said, "Should a man like me run away? Or should one like me go into the temple to save his life? I will not go!" (Nehemiah 6:11)

He realizes that a prophet who was really from the Lord would say nothing not in line with the commands of God. There was an altar of asylum in the temple courtyard to which people who were under threat could flee and be safe, but this man is proposing they actually go into the temple and shut the doors. So Nehemiah says:

I realized that God had not sent him, but that he had prophesied against me because Tobiah and Sanballat had hired him. He had been hired to intimidate me so that I would commit a sin by doing this, and then they would give me a bad name to discredit me. (Nehemiah 6:12-13)

It was all part of a plan to discourage the people from following Nehemiah's lead. Fueled by jealousy and ambition, these enemies slandered him and tried to trick him into yielding to their demands.

We must be aware of this kind of attack in our lives in these days. Do not take everyone's advice just because they are friendly to you. It may be totally wrong advice. Nothing substitutes for a knowledge of the Word of God. That is how you can detect error and tell what is wrong. The best response to such an approach is what Nehemiah uses here. He falls back upon his clear consciousness of who he is. He is a believer in the Living God and as such need not resort to trickery to save his life.

This is exactly what the New Testament calls us to as well. Faced with the normal pressures and problems of life, the Apostle Paul's word is, "Walk worthy of God" (1 Thessalonians 2:12 KJV). We are called to walk with God. You are a child of His. You belong to Him. You are therefore living at a different level than those around you.

If you remember who you are, you will not go along with these wrong things that people are being pressured into today. Henry David Thoreau wrote in *Walden Pond*, "If I seem not to keep step with others, it is because I am listening to another drum beat." A Christian also listens to another drum beat. He is following his Lord, not the voices he hears around him. Nothing will free us more from the subtle pressures and temptations of today than to remember who we are.

Always Pray

Remember Tobiah and Sanballat, O my God, because of what they have done; remember also that prophetess Noadiah [she is evidently one of the false prophets here], **and the rest of the prophets who have been trying to intimidate me.**

(Nehemiah 6:14)

Again Nehemiah relies upon the invisible hand of God, upon guidance from the Spirit. Nothing will help us more in our pilgrimage through life than to remember that the Word of God and the Spirit of God are given to us to guide us through the difficulties that come our way: Are you utilizing these resources? They are available to us just as they were to Nehemiah.

This brings us to the end of this first phase of Nehemiah's work.

So the wall was completed on the twenty-fifth of Elul, in fifty-two days. When all our enemies heard about this, all the surrounding nations were afraid and lost their self-confidence, because they realized that this work had been done with the help of our God. (Nehemiah 6:15-16)

Even their enemies had to admit that God was at work in these people's lives. He was what accounted for their amazing success. This entire project was finished in just 52 days! What a beautiful picture of the power of Christian witness in a community! Even their enemies must agree that God is at work among them.

Continuing Attacks

But the enemies are still not through. In these closing verses we see how they continue their tactics of opposition.

Also, in those days the nobles of Judah were sending many letters to Tobiah, and replies from Tobiah kept coming to them. For many in Judah were under oath to him, since he was son-in-law to Shecaniah son of Arah, and his son Jehohanan had married the daughter of Meshullam son of Berekiah. (Nehemiah 6:17-18)

That is simply saying that Tobiah had intermarried with the Israelites. Taking advantage of that relationship, he was seeking to undermine Nehemiah's influence by nothing more than mere gossip. As Nehemiah says,

Moreover, they kept reporting to me his good deeds and then telling him what I said. And Tobiah sent letters to intimidate me. (Nehemiah 6:19)

The truth that this conveys to us is that the devil never quits. He is never going to give up while we are still alive. God has wonderful blessings and much encouragement and joy for us along the way, but we must never cease battling against the world, the flesh and the devil until we get home. Do not expect your retirement days to be without difficulty or struggle. That is what the world seeks. That is their confused and distorted view of life. But it is not ours. The enemies will never quit. If they cannot undermine us with fear and flattery, they will try gossip and false rumors. This is what Nehemiah demonstrates for us.

Continue On Guard

We come now to Nehemiah 7, which is the longest chapter in the book. Here Nehemiah seeks to perpetuate the achievements that he has brought about, by appointing wise successors and establishing sound policies.

After the wall had been rebuilt and I had set the doors in place, the gatekeepers and the singers and the Levites were appointed. I put in charge of Jerusalem my brother Hanani, along with Hananiah the commander of the citadel, because he was a man of integrity and feared God more than most men do. I said to them, "The gates of Jerusalem are not to be opened until the sun is hot. While the gatekeepers are still on duty, have them shut the doors and bar them. Also appoint residents of Jerusalem as guards, some at their posts and some near their own houses.

(Nehemiah 7:1-3)

Though the wall was now finished, Nehemiah did not cease taking precautions. He realized that they were still subject to attack, and rather than open the gates at dawn, as most cities did, he directs, "Do not open them until the sun is hot." This would preclude any possibility of a surprise attack while the people were still sleeping. He appoints residents to stand guard at the vulnerable points of the wall.

This is teaching us that we must never let down our guard. How many men of prominence in the Christian life have we seen fall in their later years because they let down their guard and ceased to do battle with the enemy!

Maintaining Purity

The rest of the chapter is given over to preserving the purity of the doctrine that God has taught, and the commitment of the Jews to the cause. It was necessary to ensure that only true Israelites lived within Jerusalem.

Now the city was large and spacious, but there were few people in it, and the houses had not yet been rebuilt. So my God put it into my heart to assemble the nobles, the officials and the common people for registration by families. I found the genealogical record of those who had been the first to return. This is what I found written there.

(Nehemiah 7:4-5)

There follows a list of names of all the families of those who came back from Persia to Jerusalem under the leadership of Ezra, some thirty years before. These, of course, were among the ones who helped him build the wall. He is not only giving credit to them but is also recognizing that they will be responsible to carry on what he has begun. So having appointed leaders who would succeed him, men of integrity, courage and faithfulness, he now sees to it that their followers are also true Israelites. From Nehemiah 7:6-60 we have a list of the families of those who were able to prove their ancestry.

The spiritual application of that is that we need to know that we really belong to God: You will never be a successful servant of Christ, nor ever faithfully work for Him and serve Him, until you are assured that you know Him and belong to Him. This is not only necessary for leaders but for the common people as well. We all need to know our spiritual pedigree, otherwise our service will be weak and largely ineffective.

Nehemiah 7:61 lists some who could not prove their ancestry. They were therefore not permitted to live in the city of Jerusalem for they had uncertain ancestry. Then he moves to the leaders in verses 63-65. Certain ones among the priests were denied the right to minister because they could not prove their ancestry.

Many try to minister in the church of God today who are uncertain that they belong to God. I run into pastors, seminary professors, and leaders in the Christian community who do not themselves know that they are true Christians. These always wreak havoc in the churches they seek to serve.

How To Stand Strong

As we draw this to a close let us remember again the factors that enabled Nehemiah to stand against the pressures and temptations of his day. These are the same factors that will enable us to stand today:

First, he had a great awareness of the magnitude of the task that God had given him to do. He had a ministry to perform, and a life-style to model for others. He never forgot that God had sent him to Jerusalem to work and demonstrate to people how to live. That held him steady when there were pressures against him.

Then, second, he never forgot his own identity. He knew who he was. He knew he belonged to God and that he was part of His people.

Third, he was free from the influence of others. He refused to listen to every bit of advice that came along. He refused counsel from those who did not have access to the mind and wisdom of God.

And then, fourth, in a very common sense way he was careful to put into practice what he knew. How practical was this man! He sets up guards, assigns responsibilities, shares the labor, and investigates carefully. That is a great factor in his success.

Finally, fifth, above all else, he prays. He subjected everything to the wisdom of God.

One of the most helpful scriptures that has guided me throughout my life is one I learned as a young man: "Trust in the LORD with all your heart, And lean not on your own understanding; In all your ways acknowledge Him, And He shall direct your paths" (Proverbs 3:5-6 NKJV).

Do you want God directing your life? Then begin to do these simple things.

Nehemiah Lesson 6   49

Study Questions

Before you begin each day:
   a. Pray and ask God to speak to you through His Holy Spirit.
   b. Do not use other source books for your answers.
   c. Write your answers and the verses you used.
   d. Remember that the challenge questions are for those who have the time or inclination to do them.
   e. Personal questions are to be shared with the class only if you wish to share.
   f. If you desire, insert your name in the assigned verses to make them more personal.

First Day: Read the Commentary on Nehemiah 6-7.

1. What meaningful or new thought did you find in the notes on Nehemiah 6-7, or from your teacher's lecture? What personal application did you choose to apply to your life?

2. Look for a verse in the lesson to memorize this week. Write it down, carry it with you, tack it to your bulletin board, on the dashboard of your car, etc. Make a real effort to learn the verse and its "address" (reference of where it is found in the Bible).

Second Day: Read all of Nehemiah 8, concentrating on verse 1.

1. Where did the people gather?

2. What did the people want Ezra the scribe to do?

3. After the rebuilding of the wall the people wanted and needed to be instructed in God's ways. The same is true of us. After we become God's child through faith in Jesus Christ we too need to be instructed in God's ways. What does 1 Peter 2:2-3 say to us?

4. What is spiritual milk? Read Hebrews 5:12.

5. Personal: As you have been doing the study of Nehemiah you have been searching God's Word and partaking of spiritual food. Write down some area of your life where you feel that you have grown, or write what you have learned while doing this study. Share it with your group if you would like.

Third Day: Read all of Nehemiah 8, concentrating on verses 1-3.

1. Who was reading from the Law of Moses?

2. a. Read Ezra 7:6-10. Thirteen years earlier, Ezra the scribe had led a group to Jerusalem. According to Ezra 7:10 what did Ezra plan to do?

50   Joy of Living Bible Studies

    b. Was Ezra permitted to accomplish what he had set out to do? (See Nehemiah 8:1,3)

3. The people were eager to hear God's Word. How long did Ezra read on the first day?

4. According to Nehemiah 8:2-3, who were gathered to listen to the Law?

5. Read John 3:3. Who can "see" or "perceive" the kingdom of God?

6. a. Read 1 Corinthians 2:9-14. Can the "natural man," the man without the Holy Spirit, understand the things of God? What does the person without the Spirit feel about the things of God? Why? (See verse 14)

    b. Who can understand the things of God?

7. Personal: Just a surely as a monkey cannot understand the things of a human being unless somehow he could be born again as a human, so it is impossible for those who have not been born again by God's Spirit understand the things of God. Have you been born again by God's Spirit? Read John 1:12-13 and write it here.

If you haven't already why don't you receive the Lord Jesus Christ right now. Merely pray a simple prayer asking Him to forgive you and come into your life right now. Tell Him you believe He died to pay the price for your sin. Be certain to tell Him thank-you. Tell someone you're God's child by faith in Jesus Christ.

Fourth Day: Read all of Nehemiah 8, concentrating on verses 4-8.

1. What was the response of the people when Ezra opened the book (the Law of God) to read? (See Nehemiah 8:5-6.)

2. What did the Levites do in Nehemiah 8:7-8?

3. Read 1 John 2:26-27 and 2 Timothy 2:7. According to each of these verses who teaches us and gives us the understanding of God's will?

Nehemiah Lesson 6   51

4. Read Ephesians 4:11-13. What are some of the instruments God uses to teach us and prepare us for service?

5. Personal: Is there someone special God has used to teach you God's Word or to help you grow spiritually? Why not write a note to them telling them how God has used them in your life.

Fifth Day: Read all of Nehemiah 8, concentrating on verses 9-12.

1. As the people heard the law of God how did they react? (Nehemiah 8:9)

2. a. Read Hebrews 4:12-13 and 2 Timothy 3:16. Describe what the Word of God is like and what it does.

   b. Challenge: From these verses why do you believe the Israelites wept when they heard the Word of God read?

3. What did Nehemiah and the Levites tell the people to do after they had wept over their disobedience to God's law? Why were they told to do this? (Nehemiah 8:10-11)

4. Challenge: Describe what the Word of God does from each of the following verses:

   Psalm 19:7

   Psalm 19:8

   Psalm 19:9

   Psalm 19:10

   Psalm 19:11

5. From Nehemiah 8:12, why did the people celebrate with joy?

6. Personal: The Israelites were grieved over their disobedience to God's laws but rejoiced that God had given them the understanding of His Word and that they were once again in relationship with God. What about you? Are you in relationship with God through faith in Jesus Christ? Are you allowing Him to speak to you through His Word? How has He been using His Word in your life? Share this with someone this week.

Sixth Day: Read all of Nehemiah 8, concentrating on verses 13-18.

1. In Nehemiah 8:13 why were the leaders gathered together?

2. a. What did they find written in the Law of God? See Nehemiah 8:14-15.

   b. Were they obedient to what they read? (Nehemiah: 8:16)

3. a. Challenge: Read Leviticus 23:33-43 which is the portion of scripture Ezra would have been reading to the Israelites when they learned about the feast of the seventh month. According to Leviticus 23:40 what was their attitude to be as they celebrated this festival?

   b. Why were the Israelites to live in tents during this time? See Leviticus 23:42-43.

4. Read Nehemiah 8:17. What was their attitude as they celebrated this feast?

5. What did Ezra do each day of the feast? See Nehemiah 8:18.

6. a. Read James 1:25. What two actions are we to take regarding the Word of God?

   b. What will be the result?

7. Personal: Are there areas of your life where you are not being obedient to what God has shown you in His Word? Why not confess and forsake your disobedience? Ask God to help you to obey.

Nehemiah Lesson 7

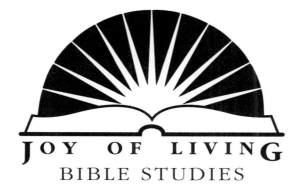

The Shining Light

In our studies in the book of Nehemiah we have seen how Nehemiah accomplished in a very remarkable way the task assigned to him to rebuild the walls and gates of Jerusalem. The point of this history, as we have already noted, is given in the Apostle Paul's word to the effect that these things happened to Israel as samples, or types, for us "upon whom the ends of the ages have come" (1 Corinthians 10:11 NKJV). These events picture the rebuilding of a life that has been damaged by sin or invaded by enemies.

Nehemiah 8 highlights the fact that after reconstruction there is a great need for reinstruction. We must learn to see life from God's perspective. We need to change the way we think about ourselves and about life. All of us have been greatly affected by the philosophy of the world, much more than we are aware. We have picked up from the media ideas and attitudes that we are hardly aware of as being wrong. We need to be reinstructed about those matters.

In chapters 1-7 of Nehemiah we saw that certain words of the Apostle Peter described what corresponds in our lives to the building of the wall: "make every effort to add to your faith goodness; and to goodness, knowledge; and to knowledge, self-control; and to self-control, perseverance; and to perseverance, godliness; and to godliness, brotherly kindness; and to brotherly kindness, love" (2 Peter 1:5-7). Adding these qualities deliberately as we live is the way to rebuild the walls and gates of a life.

Renewal By God's Word

The New Testament verse that corresponds to what we learn in Nehemiah 8 is Romans 12:2: "Do not conform any longer to the pattern of this world, but be transformed by the renewing of your mind." The instrument of that renewing is always the Word of God. If you need to change things in your life (or you are praying for someone else who does), then change must come through the knowledge of the Word of God, through the understanding of truth that was unknown before.

It is not surprising, therefore, that Nehemiah 8 opens with a manifestation of a great hunger for the Word among these people in Jerusalem.

When the seventh month came and the Israelites had settled in their towns, all the people assembled as one man in the square before the Water Gate. They told Ezra the scribe to bring out the Book of the Law of Moses, which the LORD had commanded for Israel.

So on the first day of the seventh month Ezra the priest brought the Law before the assembly, which was made up of men and women and all who were able to understand. [That would probably include teenage children, perhaps even children as young as 8 or 9 years of age.] **He read it aloud from daybreak till noon,** [Let's hear no more criticism of long church services!] **as he faced the square before the Water Gate in the presence of the men, women and others who could understand. And all the people listened attentively to the Book of the Law.**
(Nehemiah 7:73b—8:3)

Notice that this seems to be a spontaneous gathering. These people come "as one man." No invitations were sent out. No public notice was given. People were hungry for answers to their problems, for guidelines from the Word from God, and with one accord they gathered in this great square before the Water Gate. They asked Ezra the priest to bring the Law of the LORD and to read it to them. This would undoubtedly be the entire Pentateuch — the first five books of the Bible: Genesis, Exodus, Leviticus, Numbers and Deuteronomy. This indicates the tremendous desire of these people for truth. They listened, while standing, from daybreak until noon! Certainly this long attention indicates how deeply they were aware of their ignorance about life and how much they needed answers from God. They were simply crying out for the Word.

Notice that the date of this great assembly was the "first day of the seventh month" on the Hebrew calendar, which would be October 8th in 445 B.C. Notice also that Ezra the priest, the author of the book of Ezra, appears for the first time in the book of Nehemiah. Thirteen years earlier he had led a return from Persia to rebuild the temple and to teach the Law of God. Apparently he had been occupied in that task all through the time of rebuilding of the wall. But now when the people have finished their work, they are desperate to hear from the Word of God so they sent for Ezra to lead them in this.

Mark also that they gathered before the "Water Gate." You remember from Nehemiah 3 that this gate was the symbol of the Word of God — the water of the Word. This is surely an appropriate place for this gathering.

Hunger For God's Word

It seems to me that we have come to such a time as this again. The prophet Amos predicted that there would come a famine in the world for the Word of God (Amos 8:11). People would actually be starving for answers to the problems of life. Surely we have come to just such a time in our own day. I find everywhere a deep hunger among non-churched people to hear the Word of God. Wherever it is taught with any degree of understanding, they are immediately attracted to it.

In Singapore a few years ago I was invited to speak to a group of young Chinese professionals. Some 40 or 50 doctors, lawyers, engineers and others met in one of the high-rise apartments in the city. As I opened up the Bible to them I quickly discovered that they were absolutely fascinated with it. When I had to leave for another appointment, many of them crowded into the elevator with me, and others came on other elevators down to the lobby, asking questions all the way. I got in the car and as we were driving off they ran alongside, still shouting questions through the open windows. I have never forgotten that display of hunger for God's Word among people who had not yet been taught the scriptures.

When the Word is opened up, people begin to understand themselves. This is the great thing about scripture. When you know God you begin to understand yourself, because you are made in the image of God. These people in Jerusalem were soon growing in self-knowledge as they began to hunger for the Word of God. The great tragedy of our day is how few churches seem to understand this power of scripture. Across the country and around the world there are thousands of churches in which there is little life. The services are dull and dreary because the Word of God is not central.

The next verses demonstrate the centrality of the Word in this gathering.

Ezra the scribe stood on a high wooden platform built for the occasion. Beside him on his right stood Mattithiah, Shema, Anaiah, Uriah, Hilkiah and Maaseiah; and on his left were Pedaiah, Misael, Malkijah, Hashum, Hashbaddanah, Zechariah and Meshullam. [You need a seminary education to pronounce these names!] **Ezra opened the book. All the people could see him because he was standing above them; and as he opened it, the people all stood up. Ezra praised the LORD, the great God; and all the people lifted their hands and responded, "Amen! Amen!" Then they bowed down and worshiped the LORD with their faces to the ground.** (Nehemiah 8:4-6)

Clearly this is an eyewitness account of this moving assembly. I have often wondered if this has set the pattern for worship in some of the churches of Scotland. They, too, have high pulpits, at times with 20 or 30 steps leading up to them. I have preached in some of these, and it is a remarkable thing to look out at a congregation spread out below you like that. They have a ceremony there that is unique. An officer in the Church of Scotland (he is called the Beadle) comes marching down the aisle with an open Bible in his hand and all the people stand up. As he places the Bible on the pulpit they say, "Amen! Amen!" They probably learned that from this account in Nehemiah.

Then we learn how careful these people were to make clear what the meaning of scripture is:

The Levites — Jeshua, Bani, Sherebiah, Jamin, Akkub, Shabbethai, Hodiah, Masseiah, Kelita, Azariah, Jozabad, Hanan and Pelaiah [God never forgets a name!] **— instructed the people in the Law while the people were standing there. They read from the Book of the Law of God, making it clear and giving the meaning so that the people could understand what was being read.**
(Nehemiah 8:7-8)

What a marvelously clear statement of how a church service ought to be conducted! The primary business of Christians is to understand the Word of God so as to think God's thoughts after Him — to learn to think like God. Some of the scholars have suggested that the Levites were translating from the Hebrew language to Aramaic. But these languages are very similar. I do not think there would be much trouble in that respect. What they are doing, I believe, and some scholars feel is the case, is that they were breaking into small groups where people could ask questions and have them answered. They would listen to the reading of Ezra from the high pulpit and then they would gather in small groups and the Levites would spread out among the great congregation and give an explanation of the passage. Then people would ask questions about it and discuss it. It seemed an excellent way to instruct them so they clearly understood what the Word of God meant. It is not only important to know what the scripture says, it is even more important to know what it means!

The Impact of the Word

There follows a description of the impact of this upon those who heard.

Then Nehemiah the governor, Ezra the priest and scribe, and the Levites who were instructing the people said to them all, "This day is sacred to the LORD your God. Do not mourn or weep." For all the people had been weeping as they listened to the words of the Law. (Nehemiah 8:9)

Why were they weeping? It was because the effect of the Word of God is to show us what is wrong with our lives, what is creating the ruin and the disaster around us. As they listened to the reading of the scriptures they saw that the cause of their destitution and ruin lay in their own thoughts and attitudes. They saw the beauty of God and the ugliness of man. This is always the ministry of scripture to the human

Nehemiah Lesson 7

heart. They saw that the evil in society came from the pride and arrogance of their own lives.

God always lays the weakness and folly of the world at the church's door, for it is we who ought to be instructing the people. When the church does not understand itself then folly reigns in society. This is exactly what Jesus stated in the Gospel of Mark, chapter 7:

What comes out of a man is what makes him 'unclean.' For from within, out of men's hearts, come evil thoughts, sexual immorality, theft, murder, adultery, greed, malice, deceit, lewdness, envy, slander, arrogance and folly. (Mark 7:20-22)

All these things come from within. But until you hear the Word you do not realize that. That is what made these people weep. They saw their own complicity with evil.

Result of Rejecting God

I have been noticing that some of the secular commentators of our day are growing extremely frightened and disturbed about the conditions of life in America. For example, Richard Reeves, a New York columnist, wrote:

I can barely stomach the newspapers here in my hometown. In the tabloids, day after day, the first four or five pages are routinely filled with stories of parents beating or starving their children to death, of children plotting to kill their parents, of people being killed by random gunshots, of people chopping up other people, of cyanide being put in yogurt at the supermarkets.

America, I think, is out of control in some very weird ways. I don't know how bad it really is or exactly why it is happening. There are obviously many, many reasons, beginning with the unrelenting pressure of living in an open and competitive society... I don't know the answer to any of this. I suspect that things will get worse before they get better.

Observe the mood of bewilderment there, the lack of understanding of why things are going wrong. Richard Estrada, who writes in the Dallas Morning News, describes something very similar, and then comments:

More than anything else, this ugly social breakdown threatens to desensitize us as a nation. Wild West shoot-outs that kill innocent bystanders have become commonplace. Drug dealers and gang members have taken to using children as murderers. Executions of entire families by drug dealers are not unknown. Sweeps of whole communities by police bent on stopping the killing are now routine in Los Angeles.

Numbed by it all, we as a people, shrug our shoulders. Something is disastrously amiss. This is not the America most of us grew up to revere... We are demeaned as a people by this retrogression. We are less and less civilized.

Those words are not written by Christian writers. Those are the thoughts of secular commentators who see the results of rejecting the wisdom of God but they do not know to explain it. They do not know the cause of the terrible evil they chronicle.

It is only when you open the Book of God that you learn the reason for these kinds of conditions. We learn from the scriptures that as individuals, and as a nation, we have turned our backs on God's ways and wisdom. We have ignored His laws. We have missed the glory of His plan. We have messed up the beautiful world that He gave us. When we see the sad results and hear them poured into our ears continually by the media, it makes us weep, doesn't it?

Of all that is happening today, the most frightening thing is the lack of a sense of sin in society. People are doing terrible things — murdering one another, raping one another, hurting each other right and left — but they do not feel they are doing anything wrong. They have no sense of the wrongness of it. That is what the Word of God is given to correct. It awakens afresh an awareness of what is causing the wrong.

The Word Brings Joy

But though weeping is necessary and important, it is not the final message God has for us. To show this Nehemiah and Ezra speak up and correct the people.

Nehemiah said, "Go and enjoy choice food and sweet drinks, and send some to those who have nothing prepared. This day is sacred to our Lord. Do not grieve, for the joy of the LORD is your strength."

The Levites calmed all the people, saying, "Be still, for this is a sacred day. Do not grieve."

Then all the people went away to eat and drink, to send portions of food and to celebrate with great joy, because they now understood the words that had been made known to them.

(Nehemiah 8:10-12)

What a powerful statement of the effect of the Word of God! When people understand it, it brings joy. "The joy of the LORD is your strength." What a great word for grieving people who see the evil in their lives and the lives of those around them, and mourn over what it has produced! The word that brings joy is that of *forgiveness*. God can forgive! He does and He will restore. That is what Jesus meant when He said, "Blessed are those who mourn, for they will be comforted" (Matthew 5:4). I don't think you will ever be comforted until you learn to mourn. When you see the hurt, pain, and despair which sin can produce and you grieve over it, then you are ready for the comfort of forgiveness. That hurt is what is reflected in our prayer requests, listing all those painful things that people have asked us to pray about. If we mourn over them, then we shall be comforted. We shall realize, as this passage so beautifully states, "the joy of the LORD is your strength."

What does "the joy of the LORD" mean? It is the fact that God has found a solution to these problems of sin. He has found a way back to sensible, sober, wise, helpful, wholesome living. How? By learning to think like He thinks. Begin to see the world from His point of view. Listen no longer to the clamoring voices of the media. Do not take your philosophy of life from what people are saying or the advice others are giving. Listen to the Word of God.

That is the answer. It will heal your life. "He sent forth his word and healed them," writes the psalmist (Psalm 107:20). The ministry of the Word of God is to heal us and create in us a desire to share that healing with others.

Notice how Nehemiah urges the people to send portions of food to those who had nothing prepared. This is invariably the result in those who find their lives beginning to be healed by the Word of God. They start thinking of others who are hurting and want to share with them what they have learned.

Feast of Tabernacles

That way of health is dramatically demonstrated for us in the closing verses of this chapter. God had anticipated the need of these people. Centuries before, He had provided a most remarkable visual aid to remind them of the truth that would keep them from further destruction.

On the second day of the month, the heads of all the families, along with the priests and the Levites, gathered round Ezra the scribe to give attention to the words of the Law. They found written in the Law, which the LORD had commanded through Moses, that the Israelites were to live in booths during the feast of the seventh month and that they should proclaim this word and spread it throughout their towns and in Jerusalem: "Go out into the hill country and bring back branches from olive and wild olive trees, and from myrtles, palms and shade trees, to make booths" — as it is written.

So the people went out and brought back branches and built themselves booths on their own roofs, in their courtyards, in the courts of the house of God and in the square by the Water Gate and the one by the Gate of Ephraim. The whole company that had returned from exile built booths and lived in them. From the days of Joshua son of Nun until that day, the Israelites had not celebrated it like this. And their joy was very great.

(Nehemiah 8:13-17)

This is the Feast of Tabernacles, a reminder that they were called as a people out of Egypt. Their departure was sudden and precipitous. They were not even to sit down when they ate the Passover meal. They had to eat it standing, with their staffs in their hands, dressed in traveling clothes, ready to leave. They went out at a word of command, and left Egypt in one night. When they got into the desert, one day's journey out, and night fell, where were they to find shelter? Moses had been told by God that they were to collect boughs and limbs of trees, etc., and build booths for shelter. Then God ordained that they were to do this once every year. Even though later they had homes to dwell in, they were to build these booths and live in them for seven days. This was to teach them that they were always pilgrims and strangers on the earth. This world was not their home. All the great blessings of life would not necessarily be found in this present time but were waiting for them in glory. Therefore they did not need to be distressed if they did not have everything that those around them were trying to get in this life.

Hold Things Lightly

That is the truth that will deliver us from the pressures of the times. We must hold things lightly. We must not think that houses, cars, money and material gain is all that important. Even if we lack these things, the great treasures of our life remain untouched. To strive constantly to gain what everyone else has is a mistake. God teaches us to hold these things lightly. We must never forget that we are in the world but not of it. We are never to settle down here for good. I love the way C. S. Lewis has put it: "Our kind heavenly Father has provided many wonderful inns for us along our journey, but He takes special care to see that we never mistake any of them for home." We are pilgrims and strangers, passing through this world. We are involved in it, deeply sometimes, but we are never to see ourselves as a part of it.

What will enable us to remember that? Verse 18 gives us the answer:

Day after day, from the first day to the last, Ezra read from the Book of the Law of God. They celebrated the feast for seven days, and on the eighth day, in accordance with the regulation, there was an assembly. (Nehemiah 8:18)

Every day they read the scripture. Every day they saturated themselves in the thinking of God. That is what makes for realism: When you think like God thinks, you are thinking realistically. You are beginning to see yourself the way you really are. You are seeing your children, your home and your nation the way they really are. For the first time you are able to divest yourself of the illusions and delusions of a mistaken, confused world. You are beginning to work toward wholeness, healing, and strengthening of the things that abide.

If the believers of this land saw the Bible in that light, and listened attentively and eagerly to what it was saying, and learned how to conduct their lives according to the wisdom of this Word, do you think our world would be in the condition that it is today? I am sure your answer is "No." We desperately need the wisdom of the Word to instruct us how to live.

Nehemiah Lesson 7   57

Study Questions

Before you begin each day:
   a. Pray and ask God to speak to you through His Holy Spirit.
   b. Do not use other source books for your answers.
   c. Write your answers and the verses you used.
   d. Remember that the challenge questions are for those who have the time or inclination to do them.
   e. Personal questions are to be shared with the class only if you wish to share.
   f. If you desire, insert your name in the assigned verses to make them more personal.

First Day: Read the Commentary on Nehemiah 8.

1. What meaningful or new thought did you find in the notes on Nehemiah 8, or from your teacher's lecture? What personal application did you choose to apply to your life?

2. Look for a verse in the lesson to memorize this week. Write it down, carry it with you, tack it to your bulletin board, on the dashboard of your car, etc. Make a real effort to learn the verse and its "address" (reference of where it is found in the Bible).

Second Day: Read all of Nehemiah 9, concentrating on verses 1-2.

1. The Israelites were gathered together to seek the Lord through repentance and confession. In Nehemiah 9:1-2 what actions did they take to show their sorrow and repentance?

2. Numbers 33:51-55 lists the instructions given to God's people as they prepared to enter the Promised Land about 1000 years before the events in Nehemiah. What did God instruct them to do regarding the inhabitants of the land and why?

3. Judges 2:1-3 tells how Israel failed to obey. Instead of tearing down their altars and driving the heathen nations from the land they made a covenant with them. What was going to be the result of their disobedience? (See Judges 2:3.)

4. God desired His people to be holy and remain separate from the heathen nations. This was to keep the Israelites from being corrupted and led into idolatry. (Individuals such as Rahab and Ruth who were not Israelites, yet desired to serve the Lord, were to be accepted.) How does the Lord express this same principle to us in 2 Corinthians 6:14-18?

5. a. There is a difference between maintaining a casual friendship and being unequally yoked with them. Can you think of some ways a person might be unequally yoked with an unbeliever?

   b. How might this make a believer stumble in their walk or compromise what they believe?

c. Personal: Have you compromised yourself in any way? Commit yourself right now to walking with the Lord and serving only Him. Ask God to give you wisdom in dealing with unbelievers. Are there any steps you can take to correct the situation?

Third Day: Read all of Nehemiah 9, concentrating on verses 3-8.

1. What did the children of Israel do after reading the Law of the Lord? (Nehemiah 9:3)

2. They began their praise with statements of truth about God. Answer the following from Nehemiah 9:6.

   a. Is there any other Lord beside the God of the Bible?

   b. What do they acknowledge that the Lord made?

   c. Where does life originate?

3. Challenge: Read Colossians 1:15-17 and John 1:1-4 which refer to Jesus Christ. How do these verses compare to Nehemiah 9:6?

4. a. In Nehemiah 9:6 the people began their praise with who God is and what He has done in general. As they continue, their praise goes on to what God had done for them as a distinct people (the descendants of Abraham, Isaac and Jacob). In Nehemiah 9:7-8 what do they state God did for Abram?

   b. Did God keep His promise?

5. a. Read Hebrews 6:18. Does God ever lie or does He always keep His promises?

   b. Personal: How does this encourage you? What particular promise from God do you take hold of today?

Fourth Day: Read all of Nehemiah 9, concentrating on verses 9-25.

1. As the Israelites continue to praise and worship God, they recount their history and all that God has done for them. What did the Lord see and hear in Nehemiah 9:9?

2. Challenge: Read Exodus 1:1-14. Jacob (also called Israel) had taken his family to Egypt during a great famine. His son, Joseph, was already there and was in a position second only to the Pharaoh.

   a. How large was Jacob's family at the time they went to Egypt? (Exodus 1:5)

Nehemiah Lesson 7   59

   b. Why did the Egyptians enslave Jacob's family, the Israelites? (Exodus 1:6-10)

   c. Describe from Exodus 1:11-14 what their lives were like.

3. Four hundred years after the family entered Egypt, God delivers them from their bondage and promises to take them to the land promised to their forefather Abraham. They have increased in numbers so that they are now a great nation of people. From Nehemiah 9:10-11 describe God's deliverance of the Israelites.

4. After departing from Egypt it was necessary for the Israelites to travel through the wilderness to reach the land God had promised to them. How did God guide them through the wilderness? (Nehemiah 9:12)

5. Read Psalm 119:105. How does God promise to guide us?

6. Personal: We all make decisions that determine the paths we follow through our lives. Are you allowing God to guide you by His Word? Write Psalm 119:105 again, inserting your own name.

Fifth Day: Read all of Nehemiah 9, concentrating on verses 13-21.

1. What were some of the blessings God gave the Israelites in the wilderness? (Nehemiah 9:13-15)

2. How did the Israelites respond to all of God's goodness? (Nehemiah 9:16-18)

3. Challenge: The children of Israel continued to complain and rebel against God. When it came time to enter and possess the Promised Land, they doubted God and wanted to return to the bondage of Egypt. Read Numbers 14:26-31.

   a. What was the judgment they received for their rebellion? (Numbers 14:28-30a)

   b. Who was permitted to enter the Promised Land? (Numbers 14:30b-31)

4. Although that generation was not permitted to enter the Promised Land because of their rebellion, how did God deal with them during their desert wanderings? (Nehemiah 9:19-21).

60   Joy of Living Bible Studies

5. a. Read Hebrews 3:7—4:1. Why was God angry with that generation? (Hebrews 3:10)

    b. Why didn't they enter God's rest? (Hebrews 3:19)

    c. What do we need to be careful of according to Hebrews 4:1?

6. a. Personal: Read Hebrews 4:2-3. Have you entered God's rest through faith in Jesus Christ? (Matthew 11:28-30). If
       not you can do it right now. Just pray, telling God you know Jesus Christ has paid the price for your sin, and thank
       Him for forgiving you.

    b. Read Psalm 55:22. Perhaps you are no longer trying to earn salvation and are resting in what Jesus has done for
       you, but there may be some other burden you are carrying. God wants to give you rest from that, too. Make a list
       of cares and worries you are have. Give them to the Lord right now. He will take care of them for you.

Sixth Day: Read all of Nehemiah 9, concentrating on verses 22-38.

1. From Nehemiah 9:22-25, describe how God kept His promise to the children of Israel.

2. Read Nehemiah 9:26. With all of these blessings how did they respond?

3. What did God do then and how did the Israelites respond? What was the result of their response? See Nehemiah 9:27.

4. a. A cycle of blessing, rebellion, judgment, repentance and then blessing again is set up and repeated for hundreds
       of years. What do the Israelites acknowledge about God in Nehemiah 9:33?

    b. What do they acknowledge about themselves in Nehemiah 9:34-35?

5. Personal: In light of this cycle and God's goodness, the Israelites are seeking to re-establish a relationship with God.
    Perhaps you are enduring a season of God's judgment and discipline. Don't fear or be discouraged. Proverbs 3:11-
    12 tells us how we should respond to God's discipline. How do these verses encourage you?

Nehemiah Lesson 8

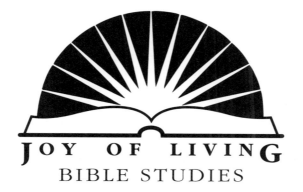

Let Us Bow Before Our Maker

The ninth chapter of the book of Nehemiah records the longest prayer in all the Bible. This prayer is a great model prayer which will teach us much for our own praying.

The first two verses record the occasion when this prayer was uttered. It follows the celebration of the Feast of Booths, or Tabernacles, which was observed in Israel for the first time for many years, following the recovery of the city of Jerusalem, the rebuilding of the walls, the resetting of the gates, and the restoring of order and some degree of prosperity to the city. That was a time of celebration but this occasion sounds a different note, as we see in the opening verses of chapter 9:

On the twenty-fourth day of the same month, the Israelites gathered together, fasting and wearing sackcloth and having dust on their heads. Those of Israelite descent had separated themselves from all foreigners. They stood in their places and confessed their sins and the wickedness of their fathers. (Nehemiah 9:1-2)

This is clearly a time of sober self-judgment. It is a time when the people expressed their feelings of shame and grief by refraining from eating, by wearing burlap (sackcloth) and placing ashes on their heads to symbolize their inner sense of desolation. They confessed their sins and their fathers' sins as well. They were aware that the evil of one generation is often passed along to the next. Many today have forgotten that this principle still applies. The cause of this sudden change in the behavior of the Israelites is not given until the end of this prayer. Let us look ahead to verses 36-37 which tell us what it was that caused them to mourn and fast, and to confess their sins. Addressing themselves to God they say:

But see, we are slaves today, slaves in the land you gave our forefathers so that they could eat its fruit and the other good things it produces. Because of our sins, its abundant harvest goes to the kings you have placed over us. They rule over our bodies and our cattle as they please. We are in great distress. (Nehemiah 9:36-37)

Here is a people that recognize clearly the connection between the evil in their own hearts and lives and the terrible conditions of slavery and bondage in which they exist.

What we see taking place in this chapter of Nehemiah is of great relevance to us. Despite our high-tech industries, our vaunted freedom from moral restrictions, our Rolex watches, Mercedes-Benzes and BMWs, we are really slaves to our materialism, resulting in spiritual emptiness today in America.

How Can We Recover?

In this prayer of the Levites in Nehemiah 9 we learn how to recover from that kind of a situation. What can we, the people of God (as they were the people of God) do to help change this condition? As we read in these opening verses, they gathered before God to pray: They fasted. They wept. They asked for mercy. They kept it all strictly within the family of Israel. They did not go outside it to involve foreigners. They did not blame others for their plight. They looked to themselves and "confessed their sins and the wickedness of their fathers." And they did one other thing, recorded in verse 3:

They stood where they were and read from the Book of the Law of the LORD their God for a quarter of the day, and spent another quarter in confession and in worshipping the LORD their God. (Nehemiah 9:3)

Three hours of confession and then three hours of praise! Thus they presented their case to God. The Levites divided themselves into two groups. Some were standing on the stairs leading up to the Water Gate and others were on a platform on the opposite side of the square. These groups were calling back and forth to the people, one group confessing the sins of the people, the other extolling the glory, compassion and mercy of God.

The rest of this chapter gives us the actual words they employ. We will let the text itself teach us how to confess sin before God and how to praise Him for His mercy and grace. It begins with a great section of praise.

Creator and Maker

First, God is praised as the Creator and Maker of everything.

Blessed be your glorious name, and may it be exalted above all blessing and praise. You alone are the LORD. You made the heavens, even the highest heavens, and all their starry host, the

earth and all that is on it, the seas and all that is in them. **You give life to everything, and the multitudes of heaven worship you.**

(Nehemiah 9:5b-6)

That is a great place to start when you are praising God. Begin with the life He gave you. It seems strange to me that men who are dependent every moment on life given to them by God, allow themselves so easily to forget that fact.

We did not create ourselves. We did not fashion this intricate machinery that sustains our bodies. Did you ever think of all the processes that are happening in your body right now that are keeping you alive, over which you have no control? That pacemaker in your mind that keeps your heart beating, for instance. You do not control that. It would be awful if you had to, wouldn't it? God sustains us moment by moment. We ought to be grateful for that. Let us never forget that our very breath comes from Him.

Caller and Chooser

Then the next section praises God as the Caller and Chooser of men. He is the One who gives undeserved blessings to those He chooses.

You are the LORD God, who chose Abram and brought him out of Ur of the Chaldeans and named him Abraham. You found his heart faithful to you, and you made a covenant with him to give to his descendants the land of the Canaanites, Hittites, Amorites, Perizzites, Jebusites and Girgashites. You have kept your promise because you are righteous.

(Nehemiah 9:7-8)

God is the keeper of promises. He is the One who initiates the call of man to Himself. The New Testament tells us that not one of us would ever seek God if He had not first sought us. It is He who awakens in us feelings and desires to draw near to Him and to find out the truth of where we came from. Not one of us would be believers today if it were not for that merciful, sovereign call of God. Jesus said, "No-one can come to me unless the Father who sent me draws him" (John 6:44). We are here today because the Spirit of God in wondrous grace has drawn us irresistibly to Himself.

Deliverer

Then they praised God as the Deliverer from sin and its enslavement.

You saw the suffering of our forefathers in Egypt; you heard their cry at the Red Sea. You sent miraculous signs and wonders against Pharaoh, against all his officials and all the people of his land, for you knew how arrogantly the Egyptians treated them. You made a name for yourself, which remains to this day. You divided the sea before them, so that they passed through it on dry

ground, **but you hurled their pursuers into the depths, like a stone into mighty waters. By day you led them with a pillar of cloud, and by night with a pillar of fire to give them light on the way they were to take.** (Nehemiah 9:9-12)

This is a retelling of the history of this nation, beginning with the call of Abraham and their deliverance from Egypt. Some of us are inclined to be indifferent to history. We should remember the wise words of George Santayana, the Spanish philosopher: "He who forgets the past is condemned to repeat it." Many have done that. We have forgotten the lessons God taught us and gone right back to do the same things over again, plunging ourselves once more into rebellion and slavery. Let us never forget that we have been wonderfully, even miraculously, delivered by the great hand of God. So the Israelites praise God for His deliverance of their nation.

The Great Provider

Then they praise Him as the great Provider of wisdom and the necessities of life.

You came down on Mount Sinai; you spoke to them from heaven. You gave them regulations and laws that are just and right, and decrees and commands that are good. You made known to them your holy Sabbath and gave them commands, decrees and laws through your servant Moses. In their hunger you gave them bread from heaven and in their thirst you brought them water from the rock; you told them to go in and take possession of the land you had sworn with uplifted hand to give them.

(Nehemiah 9:13-15)

Here is God's providential care of His own. He taught this people how to live in the midst of great wickedness. He knew He was sending them into a land inhabited by tribes that openly indulged in lewd practices, and offered their children to the god Molech by throwing them alive into a furnace of fire (see 2 Kings 23:10). It was among this people that these Israelites had to live. Yet God taught them how to avoid defilement and contamination from those things. He taught them how to be friends with these people, but not be destroyed by their immorality.

It is exactly the situation we are called to live in today. God has given us this wonderful book that teaches us the rules of life, health, salvation, deliverance and the inner strength that can resist the temptations that abound all around us (see 1 Corinthians 10:13). To neglect it is folly.

God also supplied the Israelites' needs. He gave them bread to eat when there was none. He gave them water from the rock in the middle of the desert. That is not only an account of meeting physical needs, but it describes the meeting of spiritual needs as well. The New Testament tells us these are pictures of Christ: He is the bread of life; He is the water of life. As the Israelites learned the meaning

Nehemiah Lesson 8

of these symbols they began to understand that there was coming One who would fully meet the need of the human heart. Thus they looked forward and saw the coming of the Messiah.

Confession and Praise

Now, the confessing group takes up the theme and we have an alternation between confession and praise.

But they, our forefathers, became arrogant and stiff-necked, and did not obey your commands. They refused to listen and failed to remember the miracles you performed among them. They... appointed a leader in order to return to their slavery. (Nehemiah 9:16-17a)

This is the direction rebellion always takes. When you rebel against God you invariably want to go back to the evil that you once were involved in. That is Israel did. They actually wanted to go back to Egypt, back to beatings and oppression by the heavy hand of Pharaoh, back to slaving all day, making bricks without straw. They forgot all the bondage because they longed for the sensual pleasures of Egypt. That is how rebellion deceives.

But now there follows a wonderful word of praise. It covers the history of Israel in three divisions.

1. Forgiveness at Mount Sinai

But you are a forgiving God, gracious and compassionate, slow to anger and abounding in love. Therefore you did not desert them, even when they cast for themselves an image of a calf and said, "This is your god, who brought you up out of Egypt," or when they committed awful blasphemies. (Nehemiah 9:17b-18)

Where did the impression ever arise of God as a cruel, stern God, thundering judgments upon people, demanding that they toe the mark or else be punished severely and without mercy? God is always described in the Old Testament as a God of loving care. He is compassionate and patient. He waits while people go through their trials, hoping they will learn lessons along the way, that they might return to Him so that He can bless them. Even as these people blasphemed God by creating this golden calf they called their god, He did not wipe them out but spared them.

2. Blessings in the Desert

Because of your great compassion you did not abandon them in the desert. By day the pillar of cloud did not cease to guide them on their path, nor the pillar of fire by night to shine on the way they were to take. You gave your good Spirit to instruct them. You did not withhold your manna from their mouths, and you gave them water for their thirst. For forty years you sustained them in the desert; they lacked nothing, their clothes did not wear out nor did their feet become swollen.
(Nehemiah 9:19-21)

Have you recently looked back on your life and counted up the providential care of God in your experience? We tend to take God's blessings for granted and concentrate our attention on what we do not have. The media teaches us that we deserve far more than we are getting. They flash shiny cars before us and say, "You deserve to be the president of your company. You deserve to take annual cruises on the Caribbean. You deserve to have a BMW or a Jaguar — maybe two of them. You deserve to live in a beautiful, well landscaped home."

But when you turn to the scriptures you see the other side of it. There we are brought face-to-face with what has actually gone on in our lives and in our hearts. Hidden behind locked doors of silence are acts of cruelty, violence, anger, thoughtlessness, immorality, child abuse, sexual abuse, and other ugly, miserable, vicious practices. God has seen all that. When we face the full picture as it really is, we learn that we do not deserve anything but death. But that is not what we get! We do not get death. That is the point. God is patient and longsuffering with us. He withholds judgment. He lets us experience some judgment in order to get our attention, but He does not wipe us out. He is a compassionate, merciful, caring, loving God.

3. Achievements by God's Hand

You gave them kingdoms and nations, allotting to them even the remotest frontiers... You made their sons as numerous as the stars in the sky, and you brought them into the land that you told their fathers to enter and possess... You subdued before them the Canaanites, who lived in the land... They ate to the full and were well-nourished; they revelled in your great goodness. (Nehemiah 9:22-25)

It is an amazing story! These people had just come out of 400 years of slavery in Egypt. They had no military training, and yet they confronted armies of well-trained pagans who were used to fighting, and swept them away. They took over great cities and won the land. This is describing the book of Joshua. When they were finished, they recognized that God had done this and they praised Him for His marvelous goodness to them.

Have you ever thanked God for the victories you have achieved in your life, your promotions that you did not expect to get, your achievements at work or in your home? Have you stopped to revel in the goodness of God? That is the right thing to do. Recognize that God is with you. God's hand is in what you do. Give Him glory for that. But the other group now comes in to give us the other side of the picture.

Disobedience, Judgment, Deliverance

But they were disobedient and rebelled against you; they put your law behind their backs. They killed your prophets, who had admonished them in order to turn them back to you; they committed awful blasphemies. (Nehemiah 9:26)

How does God deal with people who treat Him like that? After He has blessed them abundantly and given them so much, what happens when they forget to give Him glory and turn their backs on Him? The other group tells us:

So you handed them over to their enemies, who oppressed them. But when they were oppressed they cried out to you. From heaven you heard them, and in your great compassion you gave them deliverers, who rescued them from the hand of their enemies. (Nehemiah 9:27)

That is the book of Judges — the story of Israel at last brought under the rule of strangers for 20, 30, 40 years at a time. Then, as the people would cry out to God, He would deliver them every time by sending a judge. Then the confessors come in again, in verse 28:

But as soon as they were at rest, they again did what was evil in your sight. Then you abandoned them to the hand of their enemies so that they ruled over them. And when they cried out to you again, you heard from heaven, and in your compassion you delivered them time after time.
(Nehemiah 9:28)

What a marvelous picture of the patience of God! This is the way God works. He lets us taste the results of our evil. He gets our attention sometimes by letting sickness come or disaster strike. But it is only in order that we might hear what He is saying and be delivered. He warns us in order to keep us free.

God's Tough Love

One Sunday evening we invited the president of the Gay People's Union of Stanford University to come here and speak on the subject: *What the Bible says about Homosexuality.* We extended to him the opportunity to defend the position that the Bible endorses homosexuality as an alternate life-style. We told him he could say whatever he liked and bring all the literature he wanted. Although this man was the president of the Debating Club at Stanford, he struggled as he tried to present his case. He would read a passage and then say, "It really doesn't say that, does it?", and then he would turn to another passage. He went all through the Bible trying to prove his cause, but he floundered and could not get anything together.

We had made an agreement with him that when he finished one of our pastors would speak to the same subject. I remember well how graciously Steve Zeisler opened the scriptures and pointed out that when God forbids something it is not because He wants to limit us or narrow our lives. It is because He is protecting us from something that we cannot handle, something so devastating it will eat away at the vitals of our life and ruin us. We heard from the Word over and over again how homosexuality destroys human beings and turns them into something God never intended them to be. Eventually they would be locked into pain, hurt, misery, loneliness and death.

Out of that episode there came opportunity for us to reach out in compassion to those who were struggling with homosexual tendencies. We have seen a great number delivered and set free by the mercy and grace of God. That is what this passage describes — the tough love of God who will not let ruin overtake us without adequate warning.

The last dual presentation of confession and praise in Nehemiah 9:29-31 covers the rest of the Old Testament: the story of Israel's subjugations, first by the Syrians, later by the Assyrians, and finally the Babylonians. God allowed these enemies to come in to make His people see what was happening, to wake them up to the damage being done.

Confessing Their Own Sin

In the closing paragraph we find a change of pronouns. They have been talking about "they" and "them." Now we read about "we" and "our" as they begin to look at their own generation.

Now therefore, O our God, the great, mighty and awesome God, who keeps his covenant of love, do not let all this hardship seem trifling in your eyes — the hardship that has come upon us... from the days of the kings of Assyria until today. In all that has happened to us, you have been just; you have acted faithfully, while we did wrong. Our kings, our leaders, our priests and our fathers did not follow your law; they did not pay attention to your commands or the warnings you gave them. Even while they were in their kingdom, enjoying your great goodness to them in the spacious and fertile land you gave them, they did not serve you or turn from their evil ways. (Nehemiah 9:32-35)

As we saw at the beginning, they acknowledge that they are slaves in their own land and because of their own sins. This is where we find ourselves in America today. Our cities are torn with violence, strife, and drug wars of such intensity that people hardly dare go outside their homes. We are slaves in our own land. The only recovery is to do as these people did — confess our wrongdoing to God and praise Him for His compassionate mercy.

These Levites teach us how to confess. Notice how specific they are. "We did wrong. You have acted faithfully but we did wrong. We did not pay attention to your laws. We did not hear your words, etc." Some Christians think they are confessing when they say,

Lord, if I have injured any soul today,
If I have caused some foot to go astray,
If I have walked in my own willful way,
Dear Lord, forgive.

But that is not confession. There is no "if" in true confession. You do not say, "If I did this..." You say, "Lord, I did it. I failed. I turned aside. I forgot your Word. I walked in my own willful way." Then God hears, forgives and restores. That is His gracious nature. He is waiting to pardon us when the wrong of our lives is faced.

Nehemiah Lesson 8

Study Questions

Before you begin each day:
a. Pray and ask God to speak to you through His Holy Spirit.
b. Do not use other source books for your answers.
c. Write your answers and the verses you used.
d. Remember that the challenge questions are for those who have the time or inclination to do them.
e. Personal questions are to be shared with the class only if you wish to share.
f. If you desire, insert your name in the assigned verses to make them more personal.

First Day: Read the Commentary on Nehemiah 9.

1. What meaningful or new thought did you find in the notes on Nehemiah 9, or from your teacher's lecture? What personal application did you choose to apply to your life?

2. Look for a verse in the lesson to memorize this week. Write it down, carry it with you, tack it to your bulletin board, on the dashboard of your car, etc. Make a real effort to learn the verse and its "address" (reference of where it is found in the Bible).

Second Day: Read all of Nehemiah 10, concentrating on verses 1-30.

1. In the last verse of Nehemiah 9 we see the Israelites entering into an agreement with the Lord. Nehemiah 10:1-27 lists the names of some of those who signed this agreement. From verse 28, who else entered into the agreement?

2. Who do the Israelites separate themselves from and why? See Nehemiah 10:28.

3. In previous lessons we learned that the intermingling of the Israelites with the heathen nations led them into idolatry and apostasy. How is this principle stated for us in 1 Corinthians 15:33?

4. In Nehemiah 10:29-30, how do the signers bind themselves, and what are they promising?

5. Read Hebrews 2:1. What should be our attitude toward the Word of God that we have heard? What can happen if we don't pay careful attention to what we have heard?

6. Personal: When you drift in a boat you often don't even notice that you have moved. It is so easy for us to drift from walking in the light of God's truth. Take a moment now to search your heart and life. Maybe you haven't blatantly rebelled against God by doing something outright wrong, but perhaps you've just drifted from carefully and diligently seeking the Lord. He has promised that if you draw near to Him, He'll draw near to you (James 4:8). Write a prayer of commitment like the Israelites did to carefully seek to obey the Lord.

Third Day: Read all of Nehemiah 10, concentrating on verse 31a.

1. What did the Israelites determine to do regarding the Sabbath in Nehemiah 10:31a?

2. a. Read Exodus 31:12-13 and Ezekiel 20:12. Who was to observe the Lord's Sabbaths?

   b. Who was the Sabbath to be a sign between?

   c. What was it to remind them of?

3. Read Exodus 20:9-11 which is the fourth commandment. How were the Israelites to keep the Sabbath?

4. For whose benefit does Jesus say the Sabbath was made in Mark 2:27?

5. Read Hebrews 4:9-10. What has God provided for the people of God?

6. Personal: Read Hebrews 4:11 with Ephesians 2:8-9. Have you entered into God's rest by faith in Jesus Christ? If you have, write these verses inserting your own name.

Fourth Day: Read all of Nehemiah 10, concentrating on verse 31b.

1. What would they do on the seventh year?

2. a. Read Leviticus 25:1-5. Describe what was to be done every seventh year regarding the land.

   b. Read Leviticus 25:6-7. Does it appear that God would provide for them during the seventh year?

3. a. Read Deuteronomy 15:1-5. Describe what was to be done every seventh year regarding fellow Israelites. (vs 1-2)

   b. How does this differ from their dealings with foreigners on the seventh year? (See verse 3.)

Nehemiah Lesson 8   67

   c. What would be the result of obedience to the Lord according to Deuteronomy 15:4-5?

4. a. The standard Jesus gave us is far above the law. We are to be like Him. (See Matthew 5:48.) How does Luke 6:34-35 compare to the law of the seventh year?

   b. What is another word you could use for lending something without expecting to get anything back?

   c. Challenge: Write Proverbs 19:17 in your own words.

5. Personal: Have you ever loaned someone something and they didn't return it or pay back what they owed you? Are you still hurt, angry or bitter? Why don't you give whatever it is to the Lord. Make it a gift to Him. Ask Him to help you forgive that person. Write Matthew 6:12, making it personal by inserting your name and the name of the person you need to forgive.

Fifth Day: Read all of Nehemiah 10, concentrating on verses 32-37.

1. a. What did the Israelites assume responsibility for in Nehemiah 10:32?

   b. What was this to be used for? (Nehemiah 10:33)

2. a. The responsibilities they assumed were required by the Law of Moses (see Exodus 25—30) so that the offerings and sacrifices could be maintained year after year. Read Hebrews 10:1-4. What were the sacrifices a reminder of? (See Hebrews 10:3.)

   b. Were those sacrifices able to cleanse them from sin? See Hebrews 10:4.

   c. What were those sacrifices a shadow of? See Hebrews 10:1a.

3. What was to be brought to the Lord? See Nehemiah 10:35-37.

4. Challenge: Read Exodus 13:11-15. Why did the firstborn belong to the Lord?

68   Joy of Living Bible Studies

5. a. These sacrifices and offerings never allowed them to forget the cost of redemption. Blood shed means a death has occurred. 1 Peter 1:18-19 reveals to us what was to them only "a shadow of good things to come." How are we redeemed?

      b. Read 1 John 1:7. What does the blood of Jesus Christ do for us who believe?

6. Personal: What blessings we have! Not only do we "know" what was only a "shadow" to the Israelites, we can experience the peace that comes from having our sins removed. Write a prayer of praise and thanksgiving for what God has done for us and revealed to us.

Sixth Day: Read all of Nehemiah 10, concentrating on verses 38-39.

1. What were the Levites to receive in verse 38a?

2. What were the Levites to take into the store room of the treasury in verse 38b?

3. Read Numbers 18:25-31. The Levites were to receive the tithes from the people. After giving a tithe (a tenth) as an offering to the Lord what were the Levites to do with the rest? (See Numbers 18:31.)

4. What do each of the following verses say about our giving?

    1 Corinthians 16:2a

    2 Corinthians 8:2-4

    2 Corinthians 8:12

    2 Corinthians 9:6-8

5. Personal: There often seems to be either great pride or great condemnation in relation to giving. Do you struggle with condemnation because you can't seem to give as much as you think you ought to? Or perhaps you are puffed up with pride because of the amount you give to the Lord's work. Read Mark 12:41-44 and re-read 2 Corinthians 8:12. What is God speaking to you about giving in these verses?

Nehemiah Lesson 9

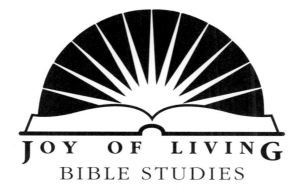

The New Resolve

"All Scripture," says the Apostle Paul in his second letter to Timothy, "is God-breathed and is useful for teaching, rebuking, correcting and training in righteousness" (2 Timothy 3:16). All of scripture, therefore, has practical application to our lives today. Whether it be a list of names as dry as dust, or a beautiful display of poetry from one of the psalms or the prophets, it all has great value for us.

Perhaps we have felt this as we have been studying through the book of Nehemiah together. We have been tracing in this book the steps to recovery from spiritual ruin or damage:

The first seven chapters tell the story of the rebuilding of the walls of Jerusalem. This teaches us how to restore our defenses — how to rebuild the walls and the gates of our lives — to close the gaps where the enemy has been getting at us, either through some outward practice or an inward attitude that has been destructive and damaging in our relationships with others.

Then, beginning with chapter 8 and on through the middle section of the book, we have been looking at the need for a change of outlook: How to renew our minds, to be reinstructed in the truth, to correct our thinking so we begin to think as God thinks. That involves a careful hearing of the Word of God. Remember the great scene of all Israel standing before the Water Gate and listening, hour after hour, to the reading of the scripture. That is what changed that nation.

As we apply this to our own lives, it also involves, as it did for them, acknowledging our past error and failure and confessing to God and praising Him for His wonderful goodness. That brings us to the natural outcome of this, which is commitment to a new life-style:

> **In view of all this, we are making a binding agreement, putting it in writing, and our leaders, our Levites and our priests are affixing their seals to it.** (Nehemiah 9:38)

There follows in Nehemiah 10:1-29 a list of the signers of this new agreement that Israel is making. First of all is Nehemiah himself, the governor, and with him a company of the priests whose names are given. Then a group of Levites, those who serve the temple, sign this agreement. Then there is a group of the leaders, the rulers or nobles of the land, and finally, the common people.

Keeping in Step With God

These people see a need for preserving and perpetuating the changes in their life-styles so as to keep in step with God; thus they sign this agreement to bind themselves to that end. This agreement represents a kind of universal urge found among humans to publicly and seriously pledge themselves to be loyal to a cause they feel is right. There are many instances of this recorded in history.

Probably the most famous document in American history is the Declaration of Independence. Our forefathers signed that great statement setting forth the reasons why they felt God was leading them to establish a new nation upon this continent. Recall its closing words:

> For the support of this Declaration, with a firm reliance on the protection of Divine Providence, we mutually pledge to each other our lives, our fortunes and our sacred honor.

History records that most of those signers of the Declaration actually did have to give up their lives. Those who did not, lost their fortunes. But all of them retained their sacred honor. Perhaps you have done something like that in your own life. There came a time when you realized you needed to make some changes in your behavior. Some of the greatest saints of the past did this. They drew up for themselves rules for their own conduct, practices they felt would help them to walk with God and to grow in grace and favor before Him. In the remainder of the chapter we find six specific commitments that these Israelites made.

Marry Within The Faith

First, they promised to avoid the unequal yoke.

We promise not to give our daughters in marriage to the peoples around us or take their daughters for our sons. (Nehemiah 10:30)

That may look discriminatory, but there is an excellent reason for that. The peoples among whom Israel was called to live practiced public lewdness. They worshipped sexual organs. Their immorality had spread diseases among their people. They killed their children by throwing them alive into furnaces of fire in worship to their god, Molech. To protect the Israelites from these dangerous practices God had told them not to intermarry with these peoples. Intermarriage would introduce into Israel attitudes and concepts that would ultimately undermine their faith and destroy them and their nation.

What is the practical application of this to us? This command is actually repeated in Paul's second letter to the Corinthians, not concerning racial distinctions, but religious. He says, "Do not be yoked together with unbelievers… What does a believer have in common with an unbeliever? What agreement is there between the temple of God and idols?" (2 Corinthians 6:14-16). Many Christians have ignored that to their own detriment by intermarrying with others of a different faith. They have thereby so undermined their own faith that evil in many ways has ultimately crept in and destroyed their marriages. Now there is no guarantee that if you marry a Christian you are going to have a happy marriage because there are other principles involved. It is certain that if you disobey this command, however, you are opening the door to much heartache, struggle and misery. There are passages designed to help people who have already done that, for God is very practical and merciful. He recognizes that for various reasons intermarriage may occur. But by and large this is practical wisdom that needs to be adhered to today. Marry those who share the same faith you have, because faith is the basis for all of life.

Rest In God's Work and Supply

The second thing the Israelites promised is to observe the seventh day and the seventh year.

When the neighboring peoples bring merchandise or grain to sell on the Sabbath, we will not buy from them on the Sabbath or on any holy day. Every seventh year we will forgo working the land and will cancel all debts. (Nehemiah 10:31)

This is a rather amazing commandment. God had said, "Six days shall you labor but on the seventh day you shall rest" (see Exodus 20:9-10). The seventh day is Saturday, not Sunday. In the past many Christians mistakenly carried the restrictions of the Sabbath over into Sunday. They even called Sunday the Sabbath. But Sunday is not the Sabbath. Sunday is the Lord's Day. It is a day for rejoicing, witness, rest and celebration. It still preserves the idea of rest for the body. The Sabbath and the seventh year are both a picture of rest. What God is teaching us is that we need rest in the midst of our activity. If you do not rest periodically your body will begin to deteriorate. You cannot maintain health by constant activity. So the seventh day is still a very wise thing to observe. But spiritually it is a picture for us of learning to rest in God at work. The Sabbath followed the pattern of creation. In six days God created the heavens and the earth and on the seventh day He rested. He no longer created. He stopped working. There is a wonderful verse in Hebrews that says, "For anyone who enters God's rest also rests from his own work, just as God did from his" (Hebrews 4:10).

What this wonderful visual aid from the Old Testament is teaching is: We are to work. We are to make decisions. We are to act. We are to make choices. But we must not forget that our activity will never be enough to accomplish what we hope to achieve. It cannot do it by itself. God must be at work in it as well. He will back up our labor and use it in ways that we could never anticipate. We do not have to worry about doing it all ourselves. We are to do what we can do and then expect God to use that. This is the repeated lesson of scripture all the way through the Old and New Testament alike. God will take our simple effort and use it in ways we could never imagine. That is the story of the feeding of the five thousand. God took a boy's simple lunch of loaves and fishes and, as Jesus prayed over it and blessed it, multiplied it until it fed five thousand people. That is the picture of one who rests in the *working* of God. That is the teaching of the seventh day.

But the seventh year teaches us to rest in the *supply* of God. God promises to supply His people's needs. We see this in Leviticus where the LORD says to Israel:

Follow my decrees and be careful to obey my laws, and you will live safely in the land. Then the land will yield its fruit, and you will eat your fill and live there in safety. You may ask, "What will we eat in the seventh year if we do not plant or harvest our crops?" I will send you such a blessing in the sixth year that the land will yield enough for three years. (Leviticus 25:18-21)

Again, that is God's way of teaching His people that we cannot do enough to supply all our needs, but He can and will. One of the great lessons taught to us again and again is: *that we are not left to our own efforts.* It is not up to us to do all the planning, programming and arranging and to supply everything. That is what the world believes. But our God is a God of supply. That is what the sabbatical year means.

Provide For Sacrificial Offerings

The third thing the Israelites undertook was to provide the money, grain and animals for the sacrificial offerings.

We assume the responsibility for carrying out the commands to give a third of a shekel each year for the service of the house of our God: for the bread set out on the table; for the regular grain offerings and burnt offerings; for the offerings on the Sabbaths, New Moon festivals and appointed feasts; for the holy offerings; for sin offerings to make atonement for Israel; and for all the duties of the house of our God.

We — the priests, the Levites and the people — have cast lots to determine when each of our families is to bring to the house of our God at set times each year a contribution of wood to burn on the altar of the LORD our God, as it is written in the Law. (Nehemiah 10:32-34)

They recognized the need for offerings and sacrifices, and that they had to continue from year to year. The

Nehemiah Lesson 9

history of Israel clearly reveals that the primary character of this nation was an emphasis on shedding the blood of animals and offering up their crops and grain to God. By so doing they were never allowed to forget the cost of redemption. Blood shed means a death has occurred. God is teaching his people that their problem with sin within was of such a serious nature it cannot be solved by merely instructing the mind. Only death can cure it.

These bloody offerings prepared the way for the death of Jesus and even our remembrance of that death at the Lord's Table. We ought to meditate on this every day. We should never allow ourselves to forget the cost of our redemption. It took all that God had to open a door that we might return to Him. As Peter put it, "For you know that it was not with perishable things such as silver or gold that you were redeemed... but with the precious blood of Christ, a lamb without blemish or defect" (1 Peter 1:18-19).

Give The First-Fruits To God

The fourth thing, and very closely related to the foregoing, was the promise of these people to bring the first-fruits of their crops, herds, flocks, and even their sons to God.

We also assume responsibility for bringing to the house of the LORD each year the first-fruits of our crops and of every fruit tree.

As it is also written in the Law, we will bring the firstborn of our sons and of our cattle, of our herds and of our flocks to the house of our God, to the priests ministering there.

Moreover, we will bring to the storerooms of the house of our God, to the priests, the first of our ground meal, of our grain offerings, of the fruit of all our trees and of our new wine and oil.

(Nehemiah 10:35-37a)

Why did they do this? Why was God so concerned about getting the *first* of everything dedicated to Him? God tells us in His original command found in Exodus:

After the LORD brings you into the land of the Canaanites... you are to give over to the LORD the first offspring of every womb. All the firstborn males of your livestock belong to the LORD... Redeem every firstborn among your sons.

In days to come when your son asks you, "What does this mean?" say to him, "With a mighty hand the LORD brought us out of Egypt... When Pharaoh stubbornly refused to let us go, the LORD killed every firstborn in Egypt, both man and animal. This is why I sacrifice to the LORD the first male offspring of every womb and redeem each of my firstborn sons. (Exodus 13:11-15)

What they are doing, of course, is recognizing the ownership and rights of God in their lives. A corresponding truth for us today is: "You are not your own; you were bought at a price" (1 Corinthians 6:19b-20a). God owns us. We do not own ourselves. These words form the central element of our Christian faith. The world says, "You are your own. If you are pregnant and you do not want the baby, you can kill it, because you have a right to do what you please with your own body." But the Bible says, "No, you are not your own. You do not have a right to do anything you like with the body God gave you."

This is true in other aspects of life as well. We are not our own. We have no right to determine what we are going to do with our lives, or even whom we are going to marry. We have certain choices granted to us, but not all choices. One of the important aspects of becoming a Christian is to recognize the rights of God, and to live our lives within the limits He establishes.

Giving Tithes To God

The fifth thing is the matter of the tithes, or the tenth part of their wealth.

And we will bring a tithe of our crops to the Levites, for it is the Levites who collect the tithes in all the towns where we work. A priest descended from Aaron is to accompany the Levites when they receive the tithes, and the Levites are to bring a tenth of the tithes up to the house of our God, to the storerooms of the treasury. The people of Israel, including the Levites, are to bring their contributions of grain, new wine and oil to the storerooms where the articles for the sanctuary are kept and where the ministering priests, the gate-keepers and the singers stay.

(Nehemiah 10:37b-39a)

It was about this time that the prophet Malachi was saying to the people, "'Bring the whole tithe into the storehouse... Test me in this,' says the LORD Almighty, 'and see if I will not throw open the floodgates of heaven and pour out so much blessing that you will not have room enough for it.'" (Malachi 3:10). This promise to pay the 10% is the response of the people to that appeal. God ordained that the tithes would be used for the support of the temple and the ministry of the Levites and the priests, in order that there might be spiritual guidance among this people.

When you come to the New Testament the tithe is no longer laid upon believers as a requirement, despite the fact that many churches teach that we are to pay the tithe today. The New Testament teaches that Christians are to give a proportion of their wealth to the Lord to recognize that it all came from Him. You are permitted to determine that proportion yourself "in keeping with [your] income" (1 Corinthians 16:2). First Corinthians 16, and 2 Corinthians 8-9 are devoted to this subject. There we are told to choose ourselves how much we can give to God. The motive is God's primary concern. We are to give as a response of gratitude for the blessings He has given us. God pays careful attention to the motive. Offerings do not mean a thing in His sight unless they are given with a cheerful spirit and from a thankful heart. They are to be used for the support of the ministry, but they are given as an expression of thanksgiving on our part.

God has ordained this as the way by which the ministry, the spiritual guidance of the church, would be supported. You give because God has first given to you. If you feel grateful for that, if your life has been changed, if you know that God has poured out blessing abundantly into your life, or stood by you in time of trial, or granted you unusual advantages, or opened doors of service and opportunity for you, or healed you when you were hurting and broken, then, of course, your heart becomes filled with gratitude, and out of that gratitude you are to give as freely as you can to the Lord. Some people can only give perhaps as little as 5%. I knew a man who gave 90% of his wealth to God all of his Christian life, and God used him greatly. But that is something we are freely to determine.

Faithfully Attend Worship Services

The final promise is given in the last phrase of the chapter: "We will not neglect the house of our God" (Nehemiah 10:39b). This is the commitment of these people to faithfully attend the worship services of the temple. All through the history of Israel the temple, or the tabernacle before that, was called "the house of God." God signified His presence there by the Shekinah Glory that was located in the Holy of Holies.

Today, under the New Testament, no building is ever to be called "the house of God." This has been ignored by the churches throughout the centuries, and temples, cathedrals, tabernacles and church buildings have all been called "the house of God." If you look to the teaching of the New Testament, however, you will find that it is not a building but the *people* who are the house of God. It is wonderful to contemplate that. Where the people of God meet together, there you have the house of God.

What this is teaching us is that we need the ministry of the saints to us all. The Apostle Paul prayed that the Ephesians may come "with all the saints, to grasp how wide and long and high and deep is the love of Christ, and to know this love that surpasses knowledge" (Ephesians 3:18-19). You cannot do that without the ministry of other people. This is of God. Hebrews has a specific admonition to that end: "Let us not give up meeting together, as some are in the habit of doing, but let us encourage one another — and all the more as you see the Day approaching" (Hebrews 10:25). The writer is referring to the return of Jesus. As we see it nearing, we need all the more to gather together because we need each other's support.

Goals for Successful Living

There, then, are the goals for successful living. That is what both Testaments teach us. Let me review them quickly for you:

Marry in the faith. Do not choose a mate who does not know the Lord. *Learn to work and live out of rest.* Learn that God will pick up what you do and use it far greater than you were able to do. Expect him to do so and rest on that fact. Do not strain or worry, and feel it all depends on you to produce success. *Frequently remind yourself of the cost of your redemption.* Do not forget the precious blood of Jesus. We are all sinners by nature. We have not done anything that can make us acceptable to God, but we have acceptance because of the blood of Jesus. *Daily remember that you are not your own.* We are responsible to the Lord to follow His guidelines, to obey His words, and to honor him. *Support the ministry out of gratitude* — do so out of a sense of blessing and thanksgiving. And, finally, *do not neglect meeting with others for mutual support, worship and prayer.* That is the way to make a success of the Christian life. How wonderfully practical it is!

Granted that it takes discipline. You will not do this casually. You cannot just shove your hands in your pockets and sing a few hymns and this all happens to you. You must decide and stick with that decision. It is not wrong to do that. Some people say that is putting yourself under law. No, it is not. It is merely recognizing the goals and the principles God has given you. That is what a disciple is — one who disciplines himself or herself.

But there is one other very important point here. Ultimately, the Israelites failed to follow through with their commitment. Subsequent history reveals that all the old sins were revived among them. The nation once again lost the blessing of God upon it. Why? We discover the key in verse 29. They said, "all these now join their brothers the nobles, and bind themselves with a curse and an oath to follow the Law of God given through Moses" (Nehemiah 10:29). They were depending on their own efforts to obey. They were saying, "We will do this or else." They were relying upon their own self-determination, their own will power. There is no expression of any need of help from God or of any provision for failure and return.

That is what the New Testament adds. It is right to vow, and to write it down for your own benefit and remind yourself frequently of your goal. But we must always add the words that Paul uses of himself, "I can do everything through [Christ] who gives me strength" (Philippians 4:13).

That is what makes the difference. Job went through some painful experiences of discipline until he learned this lesson. This is what he said: "Blessed is the man whom God corrects; so do not despise the discipline of the Almighty. For he wounds, but he also binds up; he injures, but his hands also heal" (Job 5:17-18).

Who is going to teach this generation how to live if we do not do it? That is why God calls His people to be obedient to the things that He teaches. When we do, health begins to spread over the land around us, in the community, in the family and in the home, as once again we change the circumstances of our lives in dependence on the strength of God.

Nehemiah Lesson 9   73

Study Questions

Before you begin each day:
a. Pray and ask God to speak to you through His Holy Spirit.
b. Do not use other source books for your answers.
c. Write your answers and the verses you used.
d. Remember that the challenge questions are for those who have the time or inclination to do them.
e. Personal questions are to be shared with the class only if you wish to share.
f. If you desire, insert your name in the assigned verses to make them more personal.

First Day: Read the Commentary on Nehemiah 10.

1. What meaningful or new thought did you find in the notes on Nehemiah 10, or from your teacher's lecture? What personal application did you choose to apply to your life?

2. Look for a verse in the lesson to memorize this week. Write it down, carry it with you, tack it to your bulletin board, on the dashboard of your car, etc. Make a real effort to learn the verse and its "address" (reference of where it is found in the Bible).

Second Day: Read all of Nehemiah 11:1 through 12:26.

1. What does this passage of scripture primarily consist of?

2. Read 2 Timothy 3:16. How much of scripture is given by inspiration of God?

3. How does 2 Peter 1:20-21 express this same truth?

4. a. Read 2 Timothy 3:16-17 again. How much of the scriptures are useful?

   b. What are the scriptures useful for? (verse 16)

   c. What is the purpose of the scriptures as expressed in verse 17?

5. a. Is it sometimes hard to understand how studying a list of names could benefit you spiritually? Yet, God says all His word is useful. Read Proverbs 3:5.

   b. Personal: Will you choose to believe what God says even if you don't always understand? Rewrite Proverbs 3:5 making it a personal prayer.

Third Day: Read Nehemiah 11:1 — 12:26, concentrating on Nehemiah 11:1-2.

1. What were they trying to do for Jerusalem, according to Nehemiah 1:1?

74   Joy of Living Bible Studies

2. Who was commended? (Nehemiah 11:2)

3. Read the following verses from throughout the Old Testament. Describe the attitude or willingness of each person or group to serve the Lord. Is there any difference in them?

Judges 5:9

2 Chronicles 17:16

Isaiah 6:8

Jonah 1:1-3

4. a. Read 1 Corinthians 9:16-17 in which the apostle Paul is speaking. Why does he serve the Lord by preaching the Gospel, according to verse 16?

 b. What benefit does he receive if he preaches willingly? (verse 17)

5. Read Matthew 25:40. When does this verse say we are serving the Lord?

6. Personal: After accepting Christ as Savior each one of us is called into the service of the Lord (see 1 Corinthians 12). What is your attitude as you serve the Lord? Are you like Jonah, angry and running from what God asked him to do, or are you like Isaiah, who said, "Here I am, send me?" If you've been like Jonah ask God to forgive you. Write a prayer right now committing yourself to serving God with a willing heart.

Fourth Day: Read Nehemiah 11:1 — 12:26, concentrating on Nehemiah 11:4-6.

1. The list of the descendents of Judah focuses upon one man, Perez. How many of Perez's descendants lived in Jerusalem?

2. a. Genesis 38:6-29 tells the story of Perez's conception and birth. This was prior to the giving of the law to Moses. The customs of those days were quite different than ours today. Women couldn't go out and get a job to support themselves. Why did Er die? (verse 7)

 b. Why was Onan's action wicked in Genesis 38:9-10?

 c. From Genesis 38:11,14 what did Judah think about his daughter-in-law, Tamar, and what was his plan for her?

 d. What was his attitude toward her in Genesis 38:26?

Nehemiah Lesson 9   75

3. Matthew 1:1-16 is the genealogy of Jesus Christ. Who is listed in Matthew 1:3 that we have been reading about?

4. Judah and Tamar both tried to manipulate circumstances. What do the following verses say about man's plans and schemes?

Proverbs 19:21

Isaiah 14:24

Proverbs 16:9

Proverbs 21:30

5. Read Psalm 37:7. What action does God tell you to do in this verse?

6. Personal: Do you ever try to manipulate situations and circumstances in your life or the lives of others? Why not pray about this now?

Fifth Day: Read Nehemiah 11:1 — 12:26, concentrating on Nehemiah 11:7-9.

1. How many from the tribe of Benjamin lived in Jerusalem?

2. Judges 20—21 tells the sordid history of the tribe of Benjamin, how they fell into sexual sin. Their actions were a terrible disgrace and stain on the life of Israel and God had to deal harshly with them. From Judges 20:23,35,48 describe what happened to the tribe of Benjamin.

3. In Philippians 3 the Apostle Paul describes himself. From Philippians 3:5, what tribe does the Apostle Paul come from?

4. God does not care how we started out in life or what our background is. What does Acts 10:34-35 say about God and who He accepts?

5. a. God delights in using the ordinary things and people to accomplish his purposes (for example, a tent peg in Judges 4; a trumpet and torches in Judges 7; the jawbone of a donkey in Judges 15; and a shepherd boy in 1 Samuel 17). Read 1 Corinthians 1:26-29. What does verse 26 say regarding who is called?

   b. Why did God choose each of the following:

   foolish things

   weak things

lowly and despised things, things that are not

c. Why does God use these type of things? (1 Corinthians 1:29)

6. Personal: How does it make you feel knowing that it makes no difference to God who you are, what you have, how you started out in life, what you have done or haven't accomplished, etc.? He is willing and able to use you to accomplish His purpose. Write 2 Corinthians 12:9 in your own words.

Sixth Day: Read Nehemiah 11:10—12:26.

1. This passage of scripture lists individuals and families dwelling in Israel and their various responsibilities. In each of the following scriptures what job or responsibility is listed?

    Nehemiah 11:11

    Nehemiah 11:12

    Nehemiah 11:16

    Nehemiah 11:17

    Nehemiah 11:19

    Nehemiah 11:21-22

    Nehemiah 11:24

    Nehemiah 12:24-25

2. a. How could the responsibilities listed above compare to some of the responsibilities within the Church today?

    b. Can you think of other jobs and responsibilities that you haven't already listed?

3. a. Read Romans 12:6-8. Does everyone have the same gift?

    b. What are some of the gifts listed in these scriptures?

4. a. Personal: Are you surprised at some of the gifts that are listed? Maybe you didn't think of them as gifts before. Can you think of some ways God has gifted you?

    b. Personal: Maybe you don't know what gift you have. What does 1 Corinthians 10:31 say about our service to the Lord? Personalize this verse as you write it.

Nehemiah
Lesson 10

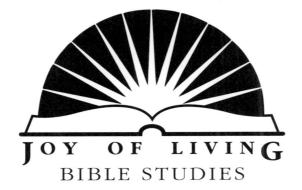

The Ways God Works

I was told in seminary never to begin a message with an apology, but I want to start this study in Nehemiah 11 and part of chapter 12 with a confession: When I first began to work on this chapter, I was simply appalled! I found it to be nothing but an unending series of hard-to-pronounce names. I kept saying to myself, "What can I do with this section?" But I am committed to two unchangeable things: One is Paul's word to Timothy, "All Scripture [*all* of it] is given by inspiration of God, and is profitable" (2 Timothy 3:16a KJV). Second, I am committed to the principle that, as an expositor, I am responsible to declare the whole counsel of God. So we are not going to skip these chapters. There are some wonderful discoveries to be made in them.

I have found in the past that whenever there is an apparently dry, uninteresting list of names in scripture, God always includes certain clues which, if you follow them up, make the section glow with light. These genealogies and lists of names look about as interesting as a telephone directory, but if you look at the clues — and they are always there — you will find some things of great interest. The more I worked on this the more I found! I now conclude that this is one of the most fascinating and profitable sections in Nehemiah. I hope you will agree with me when we complete this study.

Chapter 11 is the account of Nehemiah's actions in repopulating Jerusalem. Although the city wall has been rebuilt at this point, Nehemiah discovered that he had a problem. He had a fine, well-defended city — but without people! His solution was to draft families to move there, for a capital must be inhabited, since it is the heart of the nation. We discover this clue in the opening verses.

> **Now the leaders of the people settled in Jerusalem, and the rest of the people cast lots to bring one out of every ten to live in Jerusalem, the holy city, while the remaining nine were to stay in their own towns. The people commended all the men who volunteered to live in Jerusalem.**
>
> **These are the provincial leaders who settled in Jerusalem (now some Israelites, priests, Levites, temple servants and descendants of Solomon's servants lived in the towns of Judah, each on his own property in the various towns, while other people from both Judah and Benjamin lived in Jerusalem).** (Nehemiah 11:1-4a)

The great principle to remember in reading the Old Testament is that what happens to Israel on a physical level pictures what is happening to us on the spiritual level. Read with that principle in mind, it becomes a wonderful book of instruction. God, too, is a Builder. The New Testament tells us that He is building a city and one which has inhabitants. It is called The New Jerusalem. It is not like the old one, made of bricks and mortar, but a new city built of spiritual stones — "living stones" according to the New Testament (1 Peter 2:5). It is intended to be inhabited by redeemed people. If you draw that parallel you will begin to see some of the teaching of this passage in Nehemiah.

A Voluntary Draft

I would summarize this introductory account under the heading: a voluntary draft. The grammarians among you will immediately recognize this term as an oxymoron. That is not a specialized type of idiot! It is rather a term which contains within it contradictory elements. For instance, if you referred to a person as a "sad optimist," that would be an oxymoron. One that is very common today is, "fresh frozen food." If it is fresh, it is not frozen, and if it is frozen, it is not fresh! It cannot be both. That is an oxymoron, an apparent contradiction. Some people have suggested to me other oxymorons. "Military intelligence" was one, and "congressional ethics" was another. I will leave it to you to decide whether those qualify or not!

I hope you get the picture here. Nehemiah wants to move people into the city because Jerusalem is the center of the nation. You cannot have a capital city that is uninhabited. As the governor, he simply issued an edict: "One out of every ten people living in the suburbs must move to Jerusalem." He went through the towns and numbered the people, counting them off by tens, and then they threw a dice (actually the word is die) with ten numbers on it, and whatever number came up the man with that number was expected to move his family into Jerusalem.

But there is something very interesting here. If you read this carefully, it is apparent that when a man was chosen to move into Jerusalem he was permitted to decline if he wanted to. That is because God wanted volunteers for this. So a man could be chosen, but could decide against moving. Then the lot would be cast again and another name chosen. Sooner or later someone would be found who consented freely to go. According to the account, those who chose to go were commended by the people. They honored them because they volunteered to do what God called them to do.

We Are All Called

The application for us is obvious. The same principle applies in the church today. According to the New Testament, we are all called into the ministry — all of us! The ministry belongs to the saints! The minute you become a Christian you are moved into God's new Jerusalem. You are asked to take up labor there, to do work according to the spiritual gift God has given you. But you must also volunteer to do it. God does not force His people to do what they are asked to do. He gave us all spiritual gifts, but He does not force us to use them. Yet if you want to be respected or honored and commended at last by the Lord Himself and by all His people, then the wise thing is to volunteer to perform the realm of ministry He has opened up for you.

I stress this because in every church you will find there is a need for volunteers in various ministries. The call may have gone out, but often not enough people have volunteered. Those who have already done so, of course, are honored and commended by the people (and by God) for taking part in the ministry. Are you one of those who should volunteer today?

Beginning with Nehemiah 11:4b, our text contains two lists of names, some from Judah and some from Benjamin, the two tribes that made up the Southern Kingdom of Judah. These tribes had families that were needed in Jerusalem and there is a mingling of them. We are told that 468 men from Judah volunteered to live in the city, and 928 men from Benjamin.

Notice the list of names of the descendants of Judah focuses upon one man whose name is Perez. It concludes with the statement, "The descendants of Perez who lived in Jerusalem totalled 468 able men" (Nehemiah 11:6). When you come across a statement like that in the Bible, take a concordance and look up the name that is emphasized because God is saying something important about that person.

Perez was one of the sons of Judah (one of the twelve patriarchs who fathered the twelve tribes). The story of Perez' birth in Genesis 38 is a rather lengthy, sordid account which relates how Judah conceived this son with his own daughter-in-law. Thus it was an illegitimate birth. But following this rather shadowed beginning he went on to become one of the great heroes of Judah. His descendants are traced in almost every generation since. Even here in Nehemiah, some 400 years after Judah lived, Perez is regarded as one of the heroes of the nation.

Then, with regard to the people of Benjamin, notice that they provided twice as many men from this small tribe as those from larger tribe of Judah. The sordid history of Benjamin is given to us in the book of Judges. The last few chapters of that book tell a sorry tale of people who fell into sexual sin and began to practice homosexuality. It was a terrible disgrace and stain on the life of Israel. But two important men came from this tribe.

One is called Saul, the first king of Israel. He is a great disappointment for though he began well he ends his forty years of reign in bitter, acrimonious, angry rebellion against God. He finally takes his own life on a battlefield. There is another Saul, however, in the New Testament, who also came from the tribe of Benjamin. This is Saul of Tarsus, who is better known to us, of course, as the Apostle Paul.

What is all this teaching us? I think it illustrates what the New Testament often tells us, that God is no respecter of persons. He does not care how you started out in life. You do not wreck your chances for success in His eyes by beginning at a very low level. God can cleanse people and use them in mighty and wonderful ways. He chooses, we are told, the obscure, the once tainted, the rejects of life. He loves to pick up those kinds of people and do wonderful things with them. This is what this whole chapter is about — the revelation of how God works among His people.

God's Provision For Ministry

Nehemiah 11:10-24 is a rather lengthy section with many names. It is a picture of God's provision for ministry within the city of Jerusalem. If you have a capital city filled with people, then you need a ministry within it to maintain the spiritual strength of those people.

Priests
First, there is a company of priests selected, a total of 1,192 of them, who fall into three groups:

We are told that 822 of them "carried on work for the temple" (Nehemiah 11:12b). These were the normally officiating priests. They offered sacrifices, presented offerings, and performed the ritual that Moses had prescribed. They ministered to the spiritual life of the people.

Then there was another group of 242 who were set aside as "heads of families" (Nehemiah 11:13b). This means they had a ministry of counseling families, of working out problems and dealing with difficulties in the families of the priests. They did not neglect their own families while they were ministering to other people but these men were especially set aside to minister to the priestly families.

Then we have listed a third group of 128 men who are called, surprisingly, "mighty men of valor" (Nehemiah 11:14b, RSV). Certain priests were also warriors. They fought in the battles that Israel engaged in from time to time in defense of the city.

When we carry this over to the parallel of the church today, we find that God has also provided a "ministry within the ministry," a group of men and women who are gifted in helping people to understand the meaning of the great sacrifice of Jesus. They teach the doctrines of redemption and forgiveness of sin and help people to understand how to become and what it is to be, a new creature in Christ. Then there are others among us who are especially gifted

Nehemiah Lesson 10

in helping families understand the difficulties they are passing through and what answers there may be. Finally, there are some who especially serve as warriors — prayer warriors — and in guarding the flock from the invasion of wrong doctrines, or wrong practices that infiltrate the church from outside. So God still works the same way among us today. The whole congregation are priests (see 1 Peter 2:9), but there are some set aside to the spiritual strengthening of the others.

Levites: Outside Workers

The second division constitutes the Levites. There were 284 of them in the holy city. They fall into two groups: The first division, we read, are those "who had charge of the outside work of the house of God" (Nehemiah 11:16b).

Thank God for the men and women who are in charge of the outside work in the ministry of the church today! I am talking about deacons, as the New Testament calls them. These are men and women who are responsible to carry out various details, to take care of buildings and minister to the poor and the needy. Those who do this work correspond to the work of the Levites in the Old Testament.

Levites: Musicians

The second group among the Levites, the musicians, are very interesting. If you will look carefully, you will see familiar names among them. One name is Asaph, who is called "the director who led in thanksgiving and prayer" (Nehemiah 11:17b). Another is called Jeduthun. These two names appear frequently in the Psalms. Many of the Psalms are dedicated "to the Chief Musician," who is either Asaph, or, in some cases, Jeduthun. These two men, who lived in David's day, were chosen to set up the ministry of music within the congregation of Israel.

In 1 Chronicles 16:41 we are told that "Heman and Jeduthun" were "designated by name to give thanks to the LORD, 'for his love endures forever.'" That is the central theme of all thanksgiving. All the great hymns and praise choruses are really hymns of praise to God for His love that endures forever.

That is the great ministry of music. Music in the church is not entertainment. It is a means by which we are strengthened, fed, and helped. It is powerful, satisfying, teaching ministry. We ought to honor those who are involved in it. I have sat in the congregation during many services with tears running down my face as the musicians of the church blessed me, and strengthened me. That is what music is for. God ordained it for that purpose.

Levites: Gate-Keepers and More

Then the third group mentioned are "the gate-keepers" (Nehemiah 11:19), 172 of them. They correspond, of course, to the ministry of ushers who watch the doors. That is exactly what the word means. They are watchers who look out for people and serve them as they come to church. They help them find their seats and get their bulletins and understand what is going on. They open the windows when it gets too hot and close them again when it is cold. This is

a ministry that God Himself, through the king and the priests, had set up there in Israel.

There are still other ministries mentioned in Nehemiah 11:20-24. It speaks of "temple servants" (Nehemiah 11:21), of "the chief officer" (Nehemiah 11:22), of "singers" again "under the king's orders" (Nehemiah 11:23-24). It speaks of one who was "the king's agent in all affairs relating to the people" (Nehemiah 11:24) — troubleshooters, in other words.

Support From Outlying Cities

Nehemiah 11:25-36 lists the names of many cities of Judah and Benjamin. You may be interested that Kiriath Arba, which is mentioned there, is an ancient name for Hebron. These cities were widely scattered around Jerusalem. Beersheba, which is mentioned, was probably 50 to 60 miles from the capital city. From the coast to the Jordan valley these cities were scattered, both in Judah and in Benjamin. The Benjamite cities were north and west of Jerusalem, and the Judean cities were south and west. But all are mentioned as towns to which the capital could look for support in times of trouble.

It is easy to see how this applies to the body of Christ scattered around the world today, yet related as one body. We should all be praying for the many churches in our communities and around the world. We are not in competition with other churches. We are deriving support from them and they from us.

Heroes Of The Past

Nehemiah 12 is another list of names even more intimidating. But we are not left without some of these helpful clues. It starts right out with the words:

These were the priests and Levites who returned with Zerubbabel son of Shealtiel and with Jeshua.
(Nehemiah 12:1a)

This takes us back to the heroes of the past. Zerubbabel led the first return from captivity in Babylon to Jerusalem in 538 B.C., almost 100 years earlier than Nehemiah's day. Nehemiah is looking back at these men who led that procession. Zerubbabel was a priest and Jeshua was a Levite. They led a company of Israelites back to the city of Jerusalem to rebuild the temple. Verse 7 says that they were the "leaders of the priests and their associates in the days of Jeshua."

Verses 8-10 tell us a little more about Jeshua. By the way, that name is a variant form of Yeshua, which, if you are acquainted with the ministry of Jews for Jesus, you will recognize as the Hebrew form of the name Jesus. Here you have a Jesus in the Old Testament as well. Jeshua, we are told in verse 10, was "the father of Joiakim." The account traces his line down to the priest Jaddua.

Let me throw in a note of historic interest here: This mention of a priest named Jaddua has been the source of a great deal of criticism of the book of Nehemiah. The critics say that this dates the book further in history to the time of Alexander the Great, in about 323 B.C., which would be 100 years or so after Nehemiah lived. Josephus, the Jewish historian, tells us that when Alexander the Great led his Greek armies down through the Middle East against the land of Egypt he came up to Jerusalem. He was about to attack and sack the city when he was met by a company of priests led by the high priest, whose name was Jaddua. This man opened the book of Daniel and showed to Alexander the 8th chapter, in which it was predicted that a he-goat with a great central horn (who is clearly identified as the leader of the Grecian nation) would come against the Holy Land and conquer most of the world of that day.

When Alexander the Great saw this prediction of his own life and conquests, he was taken aback and so impressed that he spared Jerusalem and went on down to conquer Egypt and establish the city of Alexandria there. So the critics say, "This mention of Jaddua means you cannot trust the dating of Nehemiah. This is not history. This is mere legend. It is not trustworthy." But, unfortunately for that theory, the scholars have now found that there were a number of priests named Jaddua. This is certainly easy to believe because we find in this very account men passing their name on to their sons, just as fathers do today. There were several priests named Jaddua, and several governors of Samaria named Sanballat, another source of the critics' charge. So this theory is clearly unfounded.

The passage teaches us that we must not forget past heroes, the men of fame and of glory whom God has used in former days. I have been reading again the writings of some of my early spiritual heroes. For example, I am reading the book on Nehemiah by my dear patron saint, Dr. H. A. Ironside, with whom I was privileged to travel for a whole summer before coming to Peninsula Bible Church. Another hero of mine is Dr. J. Vernon McGee. This man had a worldwide radio ministry. I was his youth director for two summers and learned much from him on how to expound and bring out points of interest in the scriptures. Recently I have been reading some of the ministry of Dr. Lewis Sperry Chafer, the founder of Dallas Seminary. It blessed my heart again to see what he stood for and how faithful he was to the truth. Men like Hudson Taylor and D. L. Moody were early heroes of mine also.

I would urge you, on the basis of a passage like this, to read biography! It will bless you. It will challenge you and strengthen you to see how God has used men and women of the past to stand against the temptations and the pressures of the world and accomplish much for His glory.

Chronology

Nehemiah 12:22-26 gives the chronological time when the records that we have just looked at were recorded. It does not sound very interesting, but we are told that the first group "the family heads of the Levites ... were recorded in the reign of Darius the Persian" (Nehemiah 12:22). That meant that there was a time when they were kept as temple records but they were not actually recorded permanently until the days of Darius the Second. This would put that record somewhere between 423 and 404 B.C., somewhat later than Nehemiah. Evidently some later hand added this so that we might know when it was written.

Then there is a mention in verse 23 of "the book of the annals," i.e., the annals of the kings of Judah. One of the kings is especially mentioned in the reference to "David the man of God" (verse 24). What a remarkable influence David had! F. B. Meyer says, "How long the influence of David has lingered over the world, like the afterglow of a sunset." Yet David had a terrible record of evil in his life. He fell into adultery and was involved in the murder of his best friend, one of his generals. Because his heart was set on God, however, and he took advantage of God's provision for forgiveness, David is known to history as "the man after [God's] own heart" (Acts 13:22). If you want to learn how to live as a Christian, you would do well to study his life.

The last record is of the gate-keepers who served "in the days of Ezra and Nehemiah." That brings us to the end of the passage for this lesson.

Purpose Of This Passage

Why is all this information given to us? I think it is clear that it marks the deeds of God as part of the record of history. That is one of the great advantages of Christianity over all the other religions of the world. Most of them are religious philosophies, or simply the musings of men meditating upon various aspects of life. Many of them are a record of visions and dreams of dubious origin. But when you come to the record of the Bible, it is based upon facts. It is not legend. It is not myth. It is not fiction. It is not a record of philosophies or of the inventions of men. It is made up of historic facts. God grounds these great events in the history of the world itself.

A young Christian man told me about being confronted at work by another young man concerning his faith in Christ. This man said to him, "The Bible is nothing but a collection of myths. Men wrote the Bible. There isn't any God. Men invented Him because they wanted something to rationalize their dreams and visions. There is nothing supernatural about the Bible." The first young man answered him wisely. He said, "That is not true. You are saying that because you want to have an excuse for your own rebellion. But the truth is that these are facts. These are recorded in history. These great events took place and can be tested and proven by the records of other accounts." That is why frequently, as here in this passage, we are reminded that our faith rests upon incontrovertible evidence.

These then are the great lessons for us today. I hope you have gained something of profit and wonderful encouragement. You would not normally expect very much in these sections, but when you begin to explore, they open up much that is valuable to us.

Nehemiah Lesson 10   81

Study Questions

Before you begin each day:
   a. Pray and ask God to speak to you through His Holy Spirit.
   b. Do not use other source books for your answers.
   c. Write your answers and the verses you used.
   d. Remember that the challenge questions are for those who have the time or inclination to do them.
   e. Personal questions are to be shared with the class only if you wish to share.
   f. If you desire, insert your name in the assigned verses to make them more personal.

First Day: Read the Commentary on Nehemiah 11:1 — 12:26.

1. What meaningful or new thought did you find in the notes on Nehemiah 11:1 — 12:26, or from your teacher's lecture? What personal application did you choose to apply to your life?

2. Look for a verse in the lesson to memorize this week. Write it down, carry it with you, tack it to your bulletin board, on the dashboard of your car, etc. Make a real effort to learn the verse and its "address" (reference of where it is found in the Bible).

Second Day: Read all of Nehemiah 12:27-47, concentrating on verses 27-29.

1. What did the Israelites do after they completed building the wall?

2. Who was brought to Jerusalem to participate in the celebration?

3. What was the attitude of the people regarding the dedication?

4. Although it seemed the Israelites had worked against impossible odds, God had used them to complete the project. At every obstacle God had caused them to triumph. Read 2 Corinthians 3:5. What does the apostle Paul say about his own ability to do God's work?

5. Personal: Do you feel that the projects set before you (whether rebuilding the walls of your life or some other task) are impossible to accomplish? What does Philippians 4:13 say? Is this a cause for joy? Write Philippians 4:13 inserting your own name.

Third Day: Read all of Nehemiah 12:27-47, concentrating on verse 30.

1. To dedicate something to the Lord means to set it apart for His use. From Nehemiah 12:30 what was the first action they took after gathering together to dedicate the wall?

2. Read Hebrews 9:19-22. How was everything to be ceremonially purified and cleansed under the law?

82   Joy of Living Bible Studies

3. How are we cleansed (purified) from sin, according to the following verses?

   Hebrews 9:26-28

   1 John 1:7

4. a. Read 2 Timothy 2:19-21. From verse 20, what type of uses or purposes are listed?

   b. What must a person do to be an instrument for noble purposes? (2 Timothy 2:21)

   c. Read 1 John 1:9. How are we cleansed from our sin?

   d. Personal: What about you? Do you want to be described like the person in 2 Timothy 2:21? Is there something in your life you need to confess and turn away from? Write a prayer dedicating yourself to the Lord's use and telling Him of your desire to serve Him. Thank Him that He will help you make this change.

Fourth Day: Read all of Nehemiah 12:27-47, concentrating on verse 31.

1. After purifying themselves the leaders went to the top of the wall. What were the choirs assigned to do?

2. Challenge: Thankfulness is always part of true celebration. From our previous lessons can you recall some of the reasons they had to be thankful?

3. From the following verses write some of the reasons we have to be thankful.

   Colossians 1:12-14

   2 Corinthians 9:15

   Hebrews 13:5b

   1 Peter 5:7b

Nehemiah Lesson 10

4. Challenge: Read Romans 8:28-39. From these verses write what you as a believer have to be thankful for.

5. Personal: God has been so good to each of us. Make a list of things you are thankful for. Share the list with someone or with your class. Don't forget to express your thanks to God.

Fifth Day: Read all of Nehemiah 12:27-47, concentrating on verses 31-43.

1. There were two choirs for the celebration. Where did they march and what direction did they each take? (See Nehemiah 12:31,38.)

2. Who led the procession? (vs. 36)

3. Challenge: Ezra had returned to Jerusalem 12 years prior to this to teach the people the Word of God. How do you think Ezra might have felt as he led this great procession of people praising God?

4. a. From Nehemiah 12:43 describe the day of dedication. Who had given the people great joy?

   b. Challenge: Try to imagine what this scene was like with the choirs and musicians lined up around the wall of the city. In your own words describe this scene.

5. We have so many reasons to celebrate! Read Ephesians 5:19-20. Describe when and how we should celebrate what God has done for us.

6. Personal: Write a psalm, poem, song or letter of love to the Lord expressing your joy in Him.

84   Joy of Living Bible Studies

Sixth Day: Read all of Nehemiah 12:27-47, concentrating on verses 44-47.

1. Nehemiah 12:44 says men were appointed to be in charge of the storerooms. What was kept in those storerooms?

2. There was an abundance of contributions, firstfruits and tithes as prescribed by law. From Nehemiah 12:44b why were the people giving so abundantly?

3. The singers and gatekeepers were Levites and were to be supported by the tithes and offerings. When had the singers and gatekeepers originally been assigned these particular duties, according to Nehemiah 12:45-46?

4. Challenge: What specific duties were appointed by David to Asaph, Jeduthun, Heman and their sons in 1 Chronicles 25:1,6?

5. Read 1 Chronicles 9:23-29. What were the duties of the gatekeepers?

6. a. What does Proverbs 4:23 say we are to guard?

   b. What principles does Philippians 4:6-7 give us for guarding our hearts?

   c. Personal: Is there something you're worried or anxious about? Why don't you give it to the Lord right now and thank Him for His answer.

Nehemiah Lesson 11

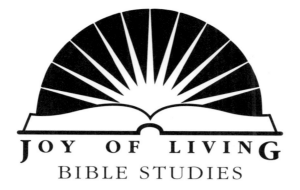

The Sound Of Rejoicing

The latter part of Nehemiah 12 tells the story of the dedication of the wall of Jerusalem. It describes a wonderful event which evidently was postponed for awhile until the city had been repopulated. In the last lesson we looked at the section that described how Nehemiah filled the city again with people. Now it is completed. The wall is built. The gates are hung. It is a well defended, beautiful city, filled with people. The time has come for celebration and the dedication of the wall.

In this section we have an account of a great procession around the top of the wall. There are choirs and musicians, and, of course, officials and politicians. You cannot get away from them. Because this is clearly a religious gathering they also take an offering. You cannot do anything religious without an offering! So the two divisions of this chapter are the great procession and the great offering.

The opening verses, beginning at verse 27, give the elements that make up true celebration.

At the dedication of the wall of Jerusalem, the Levites were sought out from where they lived and were brought to Jerusalem to celebrate joyfully the dedication with songs of thanksgiving and with the music of cymbals, harps and lyres. The singers also were brought together from the region around Jerusalem — from the villages of the Netophathites, from Beth Gilgal, and from the area of Geba and Azmaveth, for the singers had built villages for themselves around Jerusalem. When the priests and Levites had purified themselves ceremonially, they purified the people, the gates and the wall.

I had the leaders of Judah go up on top of the wall. I also assigned two large choirs to give thanks.
(Nehemiah 12:27-31a)

Here are the choirs, the instrumentalists and the singers, all gathered to celebrate the great achievement of building this wall. They were not only celebrating but they were dedicating. There are many occasions in the life of a people for both celebrating and dedicating. Recall the words of Abraham Lincoln at the battlefield of Gettysburg when he dedicated that site:

"We are now engaged in a great Civil War, testing whether any nation so conceived and so dedicated can long endure. We are met on a great battlefield of that war. We have come here to dedicate a portion of that field as a final resting place to those who here gave their lives that that nation might live. It is altogether fitting and proper that we should do so."

It is proper to dedicate. And it is proper also to celebrate when God has brought us to a place of achievement.

True Celebration

Joy

The Holy Spirit has been careful to include in this account the three aspects that make up true celebration. The first one is in Nehemiah 12:27, "The Levites were ... brought to Jerusalem to celebrate joyfully." One of the primary elements of true celebration is the expression of joy. A general attitude of joy ought to characterize all Christians.

It is amazing to me how many Christians never appear to be joyful. They are always gloomy and grim. As I have often said, they look like they have been soaked in embalming fluid! I am reminded of what a little girl said upon seeing a mule for the first time: "I don't know what you are but you must be a Christian because you look just like grandpa!" There are a lot of long-faced Christians around.

The German philosopher Nietzsche said, "If the Christians expect me to believe in their Redeemer they have got to look a lot more redeemed!" There are times of sorrow and sadness, of course, but Christians ought frequently to exude a sense of joy because they have something to be joyful about.

Joy is not the same as happiness. These people were happy, but they were also joyful. Happiness is liking the present moment because it pleases us. We are enjoying the moment and therefore we feel happy. But joy is much deeper and more long-range. Joy appreciates the past, the present, and the future, not because the circumstances are pleasing, but because the heart is right with God. That is what fills us with joy.

There is a sense of acceptance and of being valued by God Himself. Happiness therefore is basically for the moment, but joy is intended to endure for all time. Happiness depends upon happenings, but joy depends upon justification, on being acceptable in God's eyes and being co-laborers with Him. Happiness comes from without, but joy comes from within. Circumstances cannot change joy. Happiness fades quickly, but joy lasts forever.

These people were happy because the wall was finished. They had achieved their objective. But they were joyful because God had helped them to finish it. They were co-laborers with Him. His hand was involved in their labor. Aware of God's love and acceptance, they therefore were joyful and wanted to celebrate joyfully.

Purification

There is another clue hidden in this paragraph that tells us what celebration should be based on: Nehemiah 12:30, "When the priests and Levites had purified themselves ceremonially, they purified the people, the gates and the wall." Purification is necessary to celebrate. You cannot do it with a hypocritical heart. You cannot celebrate with your life in ruin. It becomes a festival of empty words. There is a need for purification.

Remember how the psalmist puts it:

Who may ascend the hill of the LORD?
Who may stand in his holy place?
He who has clean hands and a pure heart,
who does not lift up his soul to an idol,
or swear by what is false.
He will receive blessing from the LORD,
and vindication from God his Savior.
Such is the generation of those who seek him,
who seek your face, O God of Jacob.
(Psalm 24:3-6)

Many people seem to be afraid of this word, *purity*. They think it describes a goody-goody two-shoes, self-righteous kind of person. But purification in the Christian life stems from the same philosophy that motivates us when we wash dishes. You do not set your table with dirty dishes, do you? If you do, don't invite me to dinner! No, we wash dishes frequently because they ought to be clean. We do not want to serve our guests with dirty dishes. And God does not do His work with dirty vessels!

We need a periodic cleansing of our lives and hearts. This is what is manifested here. The priests and the Levites had to purify themselves, and they purified the walls, the gates and the people because they were participating in something related to God.

How do we purify ourselves? In the New Testament, it is a simple process. It is not by ritual but by confessing our faults, and believing that God has forgiven them. It is that simple. Confess your failings, your sins, your mistakes. Admit them. Do not hide them. Do not blame somebody else for them. Do not gloss them over. Confess them. Not only to God, but to any who may be involved in them. Then believe that God cleanses you, that He forgives you, that He has restored you to His favor. This is what fills the heart with joy.

Remember how simply John puts that in his first letter: "If we confess our sins, he is faithful and just and will forgive us our sins and purify us from all unrighteousness" (1 John 1:9). This word is true. So if we daily find occasions to admit our weaknesses, our faults, our ugliness, our short tempers, and our unhappy words, we can immediately receive from God the gift of forgiveness, and rise purified, to be an instrument of His working.

Thankfulness

There is still a third element in this:

I had the leaders of Judah go up on top of the wall.
I also assigned two large choirs to give thanks.
(Nehemiah 12:31)

Thankfulness is always part of true celebration. These people were thankful. You can well imagine what they were thankful for. They must have been grateful indeed for the godly leadership of Nehemiah. They were thankful for God's moving of the king of Persia's heart that permitted this whole project to come into being. They were grateful for angelic protection that watched over them as the wall was being rebuilt. They were grateful for the wisdom of God that allowed them to overcome their enemies, for the spirit of unity and cooperation that prevailed, for strength to labor, and for the supply of food and shelter. I think primarily they were thankful for the will to work, which enabled the project to be carried through to completion. This raises the question: Are we properly thankful?

Do we give thanks every day to God for the blessings we are enjoying at the moment? We are so trained by the media to grumble and complain, to insist on something we do not have, to focus on that instead of on all we do have. One of the first signs of a growing, maturing spirit in young Christians is that they begin to give thanks to God for what He has poured into their life; for the opportunities that are before them; and for the present blessings and liberties that they do enjoy. So there are the elements that make up celebration: joyfulness, purity, and thanksgiving.

A Glorious Procession

Then we learn, as this account goes on, that Nehemiah divided his choirs to march around the city.

One was to proceed on top of the wall to the right, toward the Dung Gate. Hoshaiah and half the leaders of Judah followed them, along with Azariah, Ezra, Meshullam, Judah, Benjamin, Shemaiah, Jeremiah, as well as some priests with trumpets, and also Zechariah son of Jonathan, the son of Shemaiah, the son of Mattaniah, the son of Micaiah, the son of Zaccur, the son of Asaph, and his associates — Shemaiah, Azarel, Milalai, Gilalai, Maai, Nethanel, Judah and Hanani — with musical instruments prescribed by David the man of God. Ezra the scribe led the procession. At the Fountain Gate they continued directly up the steps of the City of David on the ascent to the

Nehemiah Lesson 11

wall and passed above the house of David to the Water Gate on the east. (Nehemiah 12:31b-37)

This segment began on the western side of the wall, went down around the southern end of the city, and up onto the eastern side where they approached near the temple.

The second choir proceeded in the opposite direction. I [Nehemiah] followed them on top of the wall, together with half the people — past the Tower of the Ovens to the Broad Wall, over the Gate of Ephraim, the Jeshanah Gate [the Old Gate], the Fish Gate, the Tower of Hananel and the Tower of the Hundred, as far as the Sheep Gate. At the Gate of the Guard [which is called earlier the Inspection Gate or the Judgment Gate] they stopped. (Nehemiah 12:38-39)

These two choirs marched in different directions around the wall, circumventing the city, and joined together again on the eastern side before the Temple. It must have been a wonderful sight, with colorful banners flying, instruments playing and choirs singing.

It may have been inspired by the story of Joshua and the taking of Jericho. Joshua was told of the Lord to have the people march around the city of Jericho once a day. Then on the seventh day they were to go around seven times and the trumpets were to be blown. When they did so, the wall of the city collapsed and they were able to take it. It might also have been Nehemiah's memory of that moonlit ride he himself attempted around the city when he first arrived. He mounted his donkey but found it impossible to go clear around because the valley was strewn with rubble and ruin. That was when he saw the awesome task that lay before him. Perhaps as he remembers that he is determined to celebrate now by marching these choirs around the top of the rebuilt wall.

By the way, in the Old Testament this action of walking around an object or a piece of land is a way of claiming a certain thing for God. Abraham was told to walk around the land of promise and God would give it to him.

This raises the question, have you ever by faith walked around a situation and claimed it for God? Have you prayed your way all around every aspect of it, surrounded it in God's name, and asked Him to give it to you? This is the action today that would correspond to this event in Nehemiah.

Praise and Sharing

We next read that the choirs joined together and entered the temple for the great service of thanksgiving.

The two choirs that gave thanks then took their places in the house of God; so did I, together with half the officials, as well as the priests — Eliakim, Maaseiah, Miniamin, Micaiah, Elioenai, Zechariah and Hananiah with their trumpets — and also Maaseiah, Shemaiah, Eleazar, Uzzi, Jehohanan,

Malkijah, Elam and Ezer. The choirs sang under the direction of Jezrahiah. And on that day they offered great sacrifices, rejoicing because God had given them great joy. The women and children also rejoiced. The sound of rejoicing in Jerusalem could be heard far away. (Nehemiah 12:41-43)

What a great occasion! All the members of the various families, men, women and children, rejoicing together at what God had accomplished in their midst. The sacrifices which they offered were thank offerings prescribed by the Law as an expression of thanksgiving.

There is a correspondence to this in the life of believers today. It is spelled out in these words from the book of Hebrews,

Through Jesus, therefore, let us continually offer to God a sacrifice of praise—the fruit of lips that confess his name. And do not forget to do good and to share with others, for with such sacrifices God is pleased. (Hebrews 13:15-16)

Praise and sharing. This is the way to express our thanksgiving, joy and celebration today: praising God for what He has done and sharing with generous support and help to others around us.

A man told me about his wife who comes from another culture. When she came here she did not know anyone. She was expecting a baby, and when the baby was born a group of women from their church, without saying a word to anybody, began to bring her meals. Every night for a month they brought meals to that woman! She was greatly impressed by this willing dedication to helping her in a time of pressure. This is what pleases God, and it is what He looks for.

Offerings To God

The final account in the chapter is the great offering which was taken at the service in the temple.

At that time men were appointed to be in charge of the storerooms for the contributions, firstfruits and tithes. From the fields around the towns they were to bring into the storerooms the portions required by the Law for the priests and the Levites, for Judah was pleased with the ministering priests and Levites. They performed the service of their God and the service of purification, as did also the singers and gatekeepers, according to the commands of David and his son Solomon. For long ago, in the days of David and Asaph, there had been directors for the singers and for the songs of praise and thanksgiving to God. So in the days of Zerubbabel and of Nehemiah, all Israel contributed the daily portions for the singers and gatekeepers. They also set aside the portion for the other Levites, and the Levites set aside the portion for the descendants of Aaron.

(Nehemiah 12:44-47)

Notice three things that are especially pointed out about these offerings. Here are more of these clues that God implants in a paragraph which, if pursued, will throw light on the whole paragraph.

Give Cheerfully

We are told that these offerings and contributions were given with pleasure: "Judah was pleased with the ministering priests and Levites." The scriptures carefully inform us that offerings mean nothing if they are not given cheerfully. If you are not pleased as your motive for giving, God does not want your gift. He does not care how big or small it is. If all you are after is to make an impression on others by the size of your gift, God is not interested in that. Jesus told of a widow who put in two tiny pieces of money into the treasury, saying that she had given more than all that the rich people had cast in that day. God would pick up that insignificant amount and use it more mightily than He would the larger gifts of the wealthy. What God looks for always is a note of pleasure, of delight, of cheerfully returning funds to him out of a thankful heart.

My dear friend and patron Dr. H. A. Ironside used to tell the story of an old Scotsman who inadvertently dropped a gold sovereign in the collection bag at a church service. In Scotland, when they take up the offering the ushers use a long pole with a bag on the end of it which they pass among the pews. This old Scotsman put in a gold sovereign by mistake when he meant to put in only a shilling. As soon as he realized his mistake he tried to retrieve his sovereign. But the usher pulled the bag back and said, "Nah, once in, always in!" The old man said, "Ah weel, I'll get credit for it in glory." The usher replied, "Nah, you'll get credit for the shilling!" That is all the old man intended to give. So we are to give as God has given, freely and gladly.

Serve With Pure Motives

There is a second clue here that states that these offerings were given "according to the command of David and his son Solomon." David and Solomon lived 500 years before Nehemiah, so here is something that had been passed along through the centuries and had become a tradition by the time Nehemiah led this celebration. But it was a good tradition. It included, as we are told here, the requirement for the singers and the gatekeepers also to perform the service of purification. The ushers (gatekeepers), the instrumentalists, the musicians and the soloists all were to be purified before they performed. They were to be sure that they were not pleasing themselves or performing to get attention. They needed to be cleansed from selfish ambition and self-aggrandizement. People in the public eye can easily be tempted to act from a wrong motive. This speaks of the need for each one who ministers today to purify his or her motives before performing.

What a great tradition that is! I have been grateful through the years for the preponderance of musicians and soloists that have ministered in my own church out of a sense of love and for the glory of God. This service of purification, which was a traditional thing, looked back to the fears of David and Solomon that someone would misuse the service they were called to minister in for their own glory.

The Oneness of People of Faith

Then there is still a third point made, in the closing sentence of this paragraph. It says, "They also set aside the portion for the other Levites." They were careful to take care of others who were not able to be there, or who were busy performing and therefore did not have opportunity to share in the offerings. Whatever the reason, they recognized that they deserved a part of the offering as well.

This is a beautiful picture of the oneness of the nation Israel. God was constantly seeking to teach these people that they belonged to each other. They were not individualists, doing their own thing, but they were workers together with God. I do not know any truth that is more important in the body of Christ than to recognize that God uses people different than we are. They have different gifts and yet He uses them. We need to appreciate them for that. We must recognize that our way of serving God is not the only way but that we belong to and need one another. We need more emphasis today on how important other Christians are to us.

There is a modern parable called *The Carpenter's Tools*:

Brother Hammer, because he was too noisy, was asked by the other tools to leave the shop. But he said, "If I am to leave this carpenter's shop, Brother Drill must go too. He is so insignificant that he makes very little impression." Brother Drill arose and said, "All right, but Brother Screw must also go. You have to turn him around again and again to get him anywhere." Brother Screw responded, "If you wish, I will go, but Brother Plane must leave also. All his work is on the surface; there is no depth to it." Brother Plane replied, "Well, Brother Rule will have to withdraw if I do, for he is always measuring folks as though he were the only one who is right." Brother Rule complained against Brother Sandpaper, saying, "I just don't care; he is rougher than he ought to be. He is always rubbing people the wrong way."

In the midst of the discussion, the Carpenter of Nazareth walked in to perform His day's work. He put on His apron and went to the bench to make a pulpit from which to preach the gospel to the poor. He employed the screw, the drill, the sandpaper, the saw, the hammer, the plane and all the other tools.

After the days' work was over and the pulpit was finished, Brother Saw arose and said, "Brethren, I perceive that all of us are laborers together with God."

And so we are! We ought to take special care to recognize that mutual cooperation and mutual support of one another is part of the service of celebration. So let us celebrate with joy, in purity, and with thanksgiving unto God!

Nehemiah Lesson 11

Study Questions

Before you begin each day:
   a. Pray and ask God to speak to you through His Holy Spirit.
   b. Do not use other source books for your answers.
   c. Write your answers and the verses you used.
   d. Remember that the challenge questions are for those who have the time or inclination to do them.
   e. Personal questions are to be shared with the class only if you wish to share.
   f. If you desire, insert your name in the assigned verses to make them more personal.

First Day: Read the Commentary on Nehemiah 12:27-47.

1. What meaningful or new thought did you find in the notes on Nehemiah 12:27-47, or from your teacher's lecture? What personal application did you choose to apply to your life?

2. Look for a verse in the lesson to memorize this week. Write it down, carry it with you, tack it to your bulletin board, on the dashboard of your car, etc. Make a real effort to learn the verse and its "address" (reference of where it is found in the Bible).

Second Day: Read all of Nehemiah 13, concentrating on verses 1-2.

1. The Book of Moses included the first five books of our Bible. What did God's people find written in the Book of Moses? (See Nehemiah 13:1.)

2. From Nehemiah 13:2, what was the reason they were to be excluded?

3. a. Read Genesis 19:28-38. Who were the Moabites and the Ammonites?

   b. Read Genesis 11:31. Were the Moabites and the Ammonites related to the Israelites?

4. Challenge: Read Numbers 22-24. Summarize what happened when the Israelites neared the land of the Moabites as they journeyed from Egypt to the Promised Land.

90   Joy of Living Bible Studies

5. Read Deuteronomy 23:3-5. This is the passage of scripture that God's people were reading in Nehemiah 13:1-2. What did God do regarding the curse, and why did He do this? (See Deuteronomy 23:5.)

6. a. Read in Deuteronomy 2:9,19 what God told the Israelites on their way to the Promised Land.

   b. God told the Israelites not to provoke the Ammonites and Moabites to war, not to harass them or take their land even though He knew how they would treat Israel. God even turned their curses into a blessing. Read Proverbs 20:22. How should we respond to those who do us wrong? What will God do?

   c. Personal: God turns even that which is meant for evil into good for those who are His. Are you sometimes fearful of what others may plot against you, perhaps even those in your own family? God turned a curse into a blessing for His people because He loved them. Remember, God loves you so much that He gave His only Son for you (see John 3:16). Read Romans 8:31. How does this make you feel?

Third Day: Read all of Nehemiah 13, concentrating on verse 3.

1. What did the people do when they heard this law?

2. What does Jesus say in John 14:15?

3. a. Read John 14:21-24. According to verse 21a who loves the Lord?

   b. From verse 21b what blessing will be given to the one who obeys the Lord?

   c. From verse 24 what are the actions of the person who does not love the Lord?

4. Personal: What about you? Do you say that you love God? Do you seek to please Him and obey what He says? Write John 14:23 inserting your own name.

Nehemiah Lesson 11

Fourth Day: Read all of Nehemiah 13, concentrating on verses 4-5.

1. Who had been put in charge of the storerooms of the house of God?

2. Who was this man closely associated with?

3. a. Read Nehemiah 2:10. Who was Tobiah?

   b. How did he feel about the Israelites?

4. a. What had been given to Tobiah? See Nehemiah 13:5.

   b. What was the intended use of the room given to Tobiah?

5. This room in the temple (the dwelling place of God in the Old Testament) that was intended for the use of God's servants was actually given over to the enemy of God's people. In the following verses, the apostle Paul is writing to Christians. Who is the temple or dwelling place of God now?

   1 Corinthians 3:16

   1 Corinthians 6:19

6. Personal: Are you a temple of the Holy Spirit? Have you been born again by God's Spirit by putting your faith in Jesus Christ? (See John 3:3-16.) If not, why don't you do it right now. Write a prayer thanking Him.

Fifth Day: Read all of Nehemiah 13, concentrating on verses 6-9.

1. According to Nehemiah 13:6, when did this portion of scripture take place? (See time line on page 8.)

2. a. Where was Nehemiah while this was going on?

   b. Was he aware of what was happening?

3. What was Nehemiah's response when he returned to Jerusalem and learned what Eliashib had done? See Nehemiah 13:8-9.

4. a. Tobiah the Ammonite, the enemy of God and His people, was actually living within God's Temple. Read Romans 8:7-8. What dwells within us that is hostile to God? What is its attitude to God's law?

b. Read Romans 8:9. Who are we controlled by if we belong to Christ?

5. a. Nehemiah threw Tobiah's belongings from the room in the temple and replaced them with the things of God. Read Colossians 3:8-14. We are the temple of God. What are some of the things of the old nature we must get rid of?

b. What are some of the godly things we must add to our lives?

6. Is there something specific you need to rid yourself of? Or perhaps there is something specific you need to add to your life. Talk to God about it right now. Possibly ask the class or a friend to pray about it with you.

Sixth Day: Read all of Nehemiah 13, concentrating on verses 10-14.

1. What had happened regarding the portions of the tithes that were supposed to go to the Levites? (Nehemiah 13:10a)

2. a. Without the support of the tithes and offerings what did the Levites and singers do? (Nehemiah 13:10b)

b. Not only were they without food, they didn't have what was needed to do their jobs. Without the tithes and offerings what happened to the house of God? (Nehemiah 13:11)

3. The temple was the place where people could worship the Lord. In John 4:23-24 Jesus is speaking. Where does He say we now worship the Lord?

4. a. By neglecting the temple, the Israelites had once again neglected the Lord. He was no longer first in the national life of Israel. It was necessary for Nehemiah to correct the matter. Read Matthew 6:33 and 22:37. What place is the Lord to hold in our lives?

b. Personal: What about you? What place does God hold in your life? Are you neglecting the Lord in any way? What steps can you take to correct the matter?

Nehemiah
Lesson 12

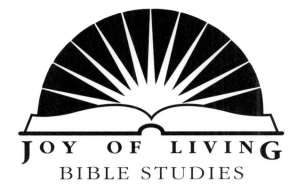

JOY OF LIVING
BIBLE STUDIES

Looking For A Few Good Men

If you like stories with happy endings you will not like chapter 13 of Nehemiah. You will probably feel that the prophet should have quit with the great celebration of the dedication of the rebuilt walls of Jerusalem. This closing chapter is really the story of a backward slide on the part of these people while Nehemiah was gone for awhile. But the trouble actually began on the very day of the dedication of the wall, while Nehemiah was still present.

On that day the Book of Moses was read aloud in the hearing of the people and there it was found written that no Ammonite or Moabite should ever be admitted into the assembly of God, because they had not met the Israelites with food and water but had hired Balaam to call a curse down on them. (Our God, however, turned the curse into a blessing.) When the people heard this law, they excluded from Israel all who were of foreign descent. (Nehemiah 13:1-3)

In Nehemiah 10, the Israelites, after a very solemn time of rededication of their lives, took a vow that they would not intermarry with the members of these other races. And yet here, some ten years later, that covenant has already been broken. Many Ammonites and Moabites are found in the congregation of Israel. They got there because Israelite men married the daughters of Ammonite and Moabite families, something which God had strictly forbidden in the Law of Moses.

You may be disturbed by this apparent case of racial discrimination on the part of Israel. Why should they exclude from their assembly the Ammonites and Moabites, the inhabitants of two countries located on the eastern side of the Dead Sea (the area which we call Jordan today)? We live in a day when no one can stand to be excluded from anything. People resent private beaches, private parks — private anything! If this happened today you can be sure there would be demonstrations in front of the walls of Jerusalem. You would see people bearing placards saying, "Ammonites and Moabites demand equal rights!"

God's Reasons Are Good

But as always in the scriptures, there was a good reason for what God was doing here. When the Israelites left Egypt they came to the edge of the Promised Land, into the country of the Ammonites and the Moabites. But these people did not offer them the normal desert hospitality of food and water. Instead, they hired the prophet Balaam to curse them. (See Numbers 22.) When Balaam was trying to ride to the hilltop to curse the Israelites, the donkey saw an angel of the Lord standing in the pathway. The beast refused to go past the angel although the prophet beat him three different times. Finally, God gave the donkey a voice and he rebuked his master: "Why are you beating me?" Then the Lord opened the prophet's eyes and he, too, saw the angel. It is a humiliating thing to be rebuked by a donkey! This is a great lesson to us. There are often times hidden reasons why God is acting the way he does. We need to be very careful that we do not violate those reasons and insist on our own way against all obstacles.

It was actually nine centuries before Nehemiah that Israel was mistreated by the Ammonites and the Moabites. Some of you must be saying, "How long does God stay mad anyhow? Nine hundred years is a very long time." This is why many critics of these Old Testament stories misrepresent the God of Israel as being vindictive and easily angered. They accuse Him of overreacting to situations like this, of cursing people for no good reason and then allowing them to remain under that curse century after century. This offends their sense of justice. But the attempt of the Ammonites and the Moabites to curse Israel reveals something about their hearts. What we often forget about God is that he is reading the hearts of men and women. He sees what is going on in our inner lives. We cannot conceal our motives and our attitudes from him. Therefore we often misjudge what God is doing because we think he is being unfair. But he is reacting to something that is much deeper. We will discover that when we check the reasons why he allowed this long-enduring curse.

A similar situation arose thirty years before Nehemiah's day. Ezra had led a group back from Babylon to Jerusalem and he, too, discovered that the people were intermarrying with these neighboring tribes, contrary to the Law of Moses:

...the leaders came to me [Ezra] **and said, "The people of Israel, including the priests and the Levites, have not kept themselves separate from the neighboring peoples with their detestable practices, like those of the Canaanites, Hittites, Perizzites, Jebusites, Ammonites, Moabites, Egyptians and Amorites. They have taken some of their daughters as wives for themselves and**

their sons, and have mingled the holy race with the peoples around them. And the leaders and officials have led the way in this unfaithfulness.

(Ezra 9:1-2)

That was a cause of great distress to Ezra. If you read the whole account, you will see that he was actually appalled into silence over this terrible violation. In the midst of his prayer that follows he adds these words,

But now, O our God, what can we say after this? For we have disregarded the commands you gave through your servants the prophets when you said: "The land you are entering to possess is a land polluted by the corruption of its peoples. By their detestable practices they have filled it with their impurity from one end to the other. Therefore, do not give your daughters in marriage to their sons or take their daughters for your sons. Do not seek a treaty of friendship with them at any time, that you may be strong and eat the good things of the land and leave it to your children as an everlasting inheritance." (Ezra 9:10-12)

We see from this that there was good reason why God forbade this social intercourse with the Ammonites and the Moabites. Their practices were terribly degrading. If they were allowed to intermarry with Israelites they would interject into the life of Israel some of these detestable customs.

But there is even more to it than this. What we must never forget in reading these Old Testament stories is that God is using a kind of visual aid to teach His people, both in Israel and in the church today, some very vital lessons. These stories are indicating something going on within — and not only among the Israelites but in the church as well. The Apostle Paul tells us that "these things happened to [Israel] as examples… for us, on whom the fulfillment of the ages has come" (1 Corinthians 10:11).

What These Stories Reveal

What do these stories reveal is happening with us? If you trace the Ammonites and the Moabites back to their beginnings, you will discover that they are relatives of Israel. Ammon and Moab, the founders of these countries, were the sons of Lot, the nephew of Abraham. During the destruction of the cities of Sodom and Gomorrah, as the fire and brimstone was raining down upon these wicked cities, angels led Lot and his family up onto the mountain-side. Lot's wife looked back and was turned into a pillar of salt, but Lot and his two daughters hid in a cave in the mountain while the cities burned before them. It is a rather sordid tale of how these girls, evidently feeling they were the last two women left on earth, contrived to trick their father into laying with them sexually. They both conceived and bore sons. One was named Ammon and the other Moab, and they went on to found tribes and countries of the same name. So Ammon and Moab are relatives, yet they are eternal enemies of Israel.

Do you have relatives like that whom you would love to get rid of but you cannot because they are related to you? They are troublesome, obnoxious and hard to live with, and yet there is nothing you can do about them because they are relatives. That is the way Ammon and Moab were with respect to Israel. They were constantly harassing Israel, trying to corrupt them, pollute them and destroy them. But Israel was forbidden to wipe them out because they were related to them.

The New Testament tells us that we have an enemy like that. It is called "the flesh" [the "sinful nature", see Romans 7:18—8:2], the old, Adamic nature that we inherited when we were born because we are children of Adam. The flesh is that inner commitment to self-centeredness that afflicts us all. I looked in the mirror this morning and I saw my greatest problem! It is I. This is true of all of us. There is something about us that wants to be king, wants to be lord, wants to be served, wants to be ministered to, wants to regulate everything, wants to run the world with ourselves at the center of things.

The New Testament calls this "the flesh." We would love to get rid of it sometimes because it tricks us and traps us, corrupts us and injures us. We deplore it at times and see how miserable it can make us. It leads us into hurtful actions that we repent of later. Sometimes you would like to get inside and rip that thing out and get rid of it forever. But you cannot because it is related to you. Yet we are called to live above it, in victory, while we struggle with it. We are called to overcome it, and to walk with God nevertheless. That is the struggle of the Christian life. All this is beautifully represented here in these stories.

Removing Evil

Now we get the detail of how this came about.

Before this, Eliashib the priest had been put in charge of the storerooms of the house of our God. He was closely associated with Tobiah [this is Tobiah the Ammonite], and he had provided him with a large room formerly used to store the grain offerings and incense and temple articles, and also the tithes of grain, new wine and oil…

But while all this was going on, I was not in Jerusalem, for in the thirty-second year of Artaxerxes king of Babylon I had returned to the king. Some time later I asked his permission and came back to Jerusalem. Here I learned about the evil thing Eliashib had done in providing Tobiah a room in the courts of the house of God. I was greatly displeased and threw all Tobiah's household goods out of the room. I gave orders to purify the rooms, and then I put back into them the equipment of the house of God, with the grain offerings and the incense. (Nehemiah 13:4-9)

The high priest had allowed his grandson to marry into this Ammonite family. We learn later in this chapter that

Nehemiah Lesson 12

he had married the daughter of Sanballat, the governor of Samaria, who was an ally of Tobiah the Ammonite. Both of these were vitriolic, bitter enemies of Nehemiah. This cozy alliance led to an invitation to Tobiah to actually move into the temple itself. To make room for him the high priest took over the storeroom that was set apart for the grain, oil and incense used by the Levites in their purification and ritual ceremonies. So there were two wrongs involved. An Ammonite and his family were actually living in the temple of God, contrary to the Law of Moses; and second, in order to permit that, they had deliberately defrauded the Levites of their rights of storage.

When Nehemiah returned he went into prompt and passionate action. He threw the baggage out, fumigated the room, and returned the oil, grain and incense to their proper place. Many people feel that he overreacted. Today we do not get upset by the presence of evil and think it strange that a man should act like Nehemiah did. Read the letters to the papers, where the public has an opportunity to speak out, and you will see how infrequently outrage over evil is expressed. Nehemiah apparently loses his temper, behaves disgracefully and throws the people out with great violence.

We must remember, however, that this is similar to the incident in the New Testament when Jesus came into the temple and found it filled with money-changers making extravagant income off the sale of the sacrifices and offerings required in the temple. It was a sordid scene of commercializing the worship of Israel. Jesus made a whip and went slashing and flashing around the Temple, upsetting tables and driving the money-changers out — much to the distress of many pacifists ever since! It indicates that there is a time for drastic action, for strong stands against evil which others have indifferently accepted.

The story reveals clearly the way evil works. It invades us quietly. Before we are aware of it we have compromised ourselves and gone along with standards widely accepted around. There are times when we must take a strong stand against evil in ourselves. We must be prepared to be drastic and take often painful action to clear up the things that are wrong in our own affairs. This is certainly true today when people have gone along with the world's attitudes toward divorce, or pornography, or the use of drugs or alcohol. Many Christians shrug their shoulders and allow evil to take root in their own lives. This story pictures the way these false forces can invade our lives and take up rooms in the very temple of our spirit, polluting and destroying us in the process. Remember what Jesus said in the Sermon on the Mount: "If your right eye causes you to sin, pluck it out… And if your right hand causes you to sin, cut it off" (Matthew 5:29-30 NKJV). Take action. Do not allow these evil things to remain. Even if it takes painful effort to do so, end it! If you have allowed your heart to be involved with something that is evil and it is painful to give it up — you must give it up. That is what Jesus is saying. Bear the pain and stand firm.

Neglect Of The Temple

Nehemiah went still further:

I also learned that the portions assigned to the Levites had not been given to them, and that all the Levites and singers responsible for the service had gone back to their own fields. So I rebuked the officials and asked them, "Why is the house of God neglected?" Then I called them together and stationed them at their posts. All Judah brought the tithes of grain, new wine and oil into the storerooms. (Nehemiah 13:10-12)

When Tobiah moved into the temple and they had to throw out the grain and oil and incense that the Levites needed, it meant that the Levites had no supplies to work with. Since they could not perform their ministry, they could not even be adequately supported, so they went to work in the fields to earn a living for themselves. As a result, the services of the temple were sorely neglected. The center of their life as a nation was not being maintained.

It is similar to an individual who allows his Bible reading and his prayer time to disappear from his life. Soon he begins to live like the world around. False forces start to creep in and take over. What it calls for is drastic, deliberate action to change the whole picture. This is what Nehemiah did. He rebuked the officials, we are told. Insistent on obeying the scriptures, he calls them to account. Then he calls on the people to bring in the tithes and the oil and the incense again and to refill the temple storage areas, allowing the Levites to go back to work. Thus God's order was restored in the nation.

Be Faithful

There is still a third step here:

I put Shelemiah the priest, Zadok the scribe, and a Levite named Pedaiah in charge of the storerooms and made Hanan son of Zaccur, the son of Mattaniah, their assistant, because these men were considered trustworthy. They were made responsible for distributing the supplies to their brothers. (Nehemiah 13:13)

Notice how representative this group is that he chooses. There is a priest, a scribe, a Levite, and a layman. All four represent various aspects of the life of Israel and share one great quality. He tells us: "these men were considered trustworthy." They were faithful men. I have discovered that today faithfulness is a quality not highly esteemed, although we often pay lip service to it. It is disheartening to me at times to see how few people take seriously the responsibility to carry through faithfully what they have undertaken.

Faithfulness is the quality that God admires. Paul says that those who minister in the church are "servants of Christ and … those entrusted with the secret things of God.

Now it is required that those who have been given a trust must prove faithful" (1 Corinthians 4:1). That is the primary thing God looks for: the ability to hang in with an assignment until you are through; the willingness to fulfill responsibility year after year after year and not need to be praised or thanked or publicly encouraged in order to do so; to work unto the Lord; to show up on time and to not leave until the work is done.

Nehemiah does not look for someone who is macho or has a great personality. He looks for someone who is faithful. God honors that. Those who serve God acceptably in this life He will reward with the words, "Well done, good and faithful servant!" (Matthew 25:21).

Qualities In A Leader

I have learned through the years to look for four qualities in leaders. I look first for a searching mind: a person who is mentally alert, who has curiosity about life, who never gives up learning. Such a person is always reading, always listening, always thinking about what he or she hears and trying to reason out what is behind it. A searching mind is aware of its lack of knowledge and keeps hoping to remedy the problem by learning more all the time.

Then, second, I look for a humble heart: someone whose ego is not on the line all the time, who must be praised and honored and encouraged in order to get them to do anything at all; who gets disgruntled and turned off if they do not get recognized. I look for someone who understands that service is a privilege; that power is not conferred upon you by an office but by serving people; that becoming a servant to others is the means of awakening a sense of gratitude on their part that makes them willing to follow what you suggest. People who learn how to lead that way are always tremendously useful in God's work and in God's kingdom. Jesus himself taught us that. "He who would be greatest among you," He said, "let him become the servant of all" (see Mark 10:43-44; Luke 22:26).

Third, I look for an evident gift: God's people are gifted people. Every member of the body of Christ who has been equipped by the Holy Spirit with a special ability to do something. It is not a burden any more than wings are a burden to a bird. It is a delight to them. I look for people who have the gift for what we are asking them to do because they will stay with it and enjoy it to the end.

And then, fourth, undergirding all the others and making them possible, is a faithful spirit: someone who will not quit; someone who sees his work as a ministry of service to the Lord himself, who has undertaken it out of gratitude in his own life and heart, and no matter how tough it gets and how rough it gets, will not quit.

Isn't it marvelous as we go through this account to recognize how beautifully each of these qualities is seen in Nehemiah himself? What a great administrative gift he had! How he could organize things, put people to work and help them understand what they had to do! And yet, how faithful he was in this. Of all the people who observed the terrible ruin of Jerusalem, who knew about its walls broken down and its gates burned, it took a man far off in the kingdom of Persia to come and do something about it. At great personal cost, and at much expenditure of labor and of commitment, he came and undertook the project and carried it through. He never quit. And when the enemies gathered against him, that did not slow him down. He stayed with it, encouraging others and pressing on until the job was accomplished. That is the lesson of this book.

God looks for these kind of people to change the age in which they live. That is what we are called to do today. We are all involved in it, not just the obvious, visible leaders. The work of the ministry is going on all the time by people in their shops, homes and offices, faithful men and women who are willing to carry this through to the end.

Nehemiah's Prayer

Let us remember that when we read this prayer of Nehemiah:

Remember me for this, O my God, and do not blot out what I have so faithfully done for the house of my God and its services. (Nehemiah 13:14)

Some people think it sounds self-serving, that he is concerned that God is going to forget him and not reward him adequately. But what he is doing is recognizing his own frailty and his own tendency to self-deception. He is saying, in effect, "Lord, I have done all this but you may see it differently than I. You may see something in me that would cause you to blot this all out of your book. If you feel that way, show it to me." That is what he is asking.

It is really the same prayer that David prayed at the end of Psalm 139: "Search me, O God, and know my heart; test me and know my anxious thoughts. See if there is any offensive way in me, and lead me in the way everlasting" (Psalm 139:23-24). That is a wonderfully honest prayer. It is saying, "Lord, I do not know myself very well. I deceive myself easily. I think I am doing fine, but you may see a lot of things that are terribly wrong with what I am doing. So Lord, search me and see if there is any wicked way in me, and lead me to the point where I can see that, too."

It is a great prayer for all believers. God has placed us in a critical moment of human history. Who is going to reach the drug addicts? Who is going to reach those who are trying to climb the ladder of success, seeking to satisfy themselves by material gain and possessions? Who is going to reach the hundreds of thousands of spiritually bankrupt people all around us? They do not come to church. Who is going to talk to them? God has called us to a ministry to reach out to them. And we need God's help in doing so.

Therefore this is a call for faithful leadership that will stay with the task and see that it gets done, whether it be within the confines of a church ministry itself or touching the world around us. This is what God calls us to.

Nehemiah Lesson 12   97

Study Questions

Before you begin each day:
   a. Pray and ask God to speak to you through His Holy Spirit.
   b. Do not use other source books for your answers.
   c. Write your answers and the verses you used.
   d. Remember that the challenge questions are for those who have the time or inclination to do them.
   e. Personal questions are to be shared with the class only if you wish to share.
   f. If you desire, insert your name in the assigned verses to make them more personal.

First Day: Read the Commentary on Nehemiah 13:1-14.

1. What meaningful or new thought did you find in the notes on Nehemiah 13:1-14, or from your teacher's lecture? What personal application did you choose to apply to your life?

2. Look for a verse in the lesson to memorize this week. Write it down, carry it with you, tack it to your bulletin board, on the dashboard of your car, etc. Make a real effort to learn the verse and its "address" (reference of where it is found in the Bible).

Second Day: Read all of Nehemiah 13:15-31, concentrating on verses 15-18.

1. a. These events are taking place after Nehemiah's return to Jerusalem. From verse 15, what were the men of Judah doing on the Sabbath?

    b. What did Nehemiah do?

2. a. What were the men from Tyre doing on the Sabbath? See Nehemiah 13:16.

    b. Who did Nehemiah rebuke about this?

3. What was Nehemiah concerned about in Nehemiah 13:18?

4. Challenge: Read Proverbs 1:29-31 and describe what happens to those who refuse to learn from and obey the Lord.

98   Joy of Living Bible Studies

5. a. In Nehemiah's time the Israelites didn't learn from their past. They returned to some of the very actions that caused them to go into captivity. Read 1 Corinthians 11:31-32 and describe how the Lord deals with us.

      b. What does Proverbs 3:11-12 say about God's discipline?

      c. Personal: From these verses how can you avoid having to be disciplined? Do you want God to discipline you when you need it? Write a prayer expressing how you feel about these matters.

Third Day: Read all of Nehemiah 13:15-31, concentrating on verses 19-22.

1. What measures did Nehemiah take to keep the Sabbath holy? See Nehemiah 13:19.

2. What actions did the merchants and sellers take that show that they were persistent in trying to get God's people to disobey God's command? See verse 20.

3. What did Nehemiah have to do to get them to stop? See verses 21-22.

4. What did the Levites do before guarding the gates?

5. a. Just like the Levites, we too are to be cleansed and purified to be fit for the Master's use. What does 2 Timothy 2:21 say about this?

      b. Read 1 John 1:9. What action are we as believers to take to be purified?

      c. Personal: Is there something you need to confess to the Lord? Why not do it now, then write a prayer thanking Him for His forgiveness.

Fourth Day: Read all of Nehemiah 13:15-31, concentrating on verse 22.

1. Why did Nehemiah have the Levites guard the gates?

Nehemiah Lesson 12   99

2. There are two reasons given in scripture for the inauguration of the Sabbath. What is the reason given in Exodus 20:11?

3. What reason is given to the Israelites for the Sabbath in Deuteronomy 5:15?

4. a. From these scriptures we see there are two aspects of the Sabbath—creation and redemption. There are two corresponding forms of rest. One form is a *rest of cessation.* As God ceased from His work of creation and rested, what are we to cease from in our desire to be saved? Read Romans 4:5 and Ephesians 2:8-9 for your answer.

   b. There is also a *rest of faith,* of rejoicing in the mighty delivering power of God. From Romans 4:5 and Ephesians 2:8-9 how are we saved?

   c. Challenge: In your own words describe how these verses explain God's rest for us.

5. a. Read what Jesus says in Matthew 11:28-29. Where do we find rest?

   b. Personal: Have you found rest in Jesus Christ by putting your faith and trust in Him alone for salvation? If not why not do it now?

   c. Perhaps you are resting in the Lord for salvation but you are still burdened by worries of this life. What does Hebrews 4:16 say you should do? Write this verse inserting your own name.

Fifth Day: Read all of Nehemiah 13:15-31, concentrating on verses 23-27.

1. From Nehemiah 13:23 what had the men of Judah begun doing again?

100   Joy of Living Bible Studies

2. What result did this have on their children?

3. How did Nehemiah express how seriously he took this? See Nehemiah 13:25.

4. Why did Nehemiah take this so seriously? See Nehemiah 13:26-27.

5. Personal: Do you think that what you do affects your children?...others? Are there any areas where you have
    compromised yourself? Ask the Lord for forgiveness right now and commit yourself to walking in His paths.

Sixth Day: Read all of Nehemiah 13:15-31, concentrating on verses 28-31.

1. In Nehemiah 13:29 what does Nehemiah say had been defiled?

2. How does Malachi 2:7 describe what a priest should be?

3. As the priests were given the ministry to be the messenger of the Lord Almighty, what does 2 Corinthians 5:20 say is
    the ministry of Christians?

4. What did Nehemiah do in Nehemiah 13:30-31?

5. a. Read 2 Corinthians 9:8. What does God provide for us?

    b. Because of God's provision for us what will we abound in?

6. a. Personal: In the book of Nehemiah we have seen God's faithfulness to His people and His ability to restore, not only
        a wall, but people to a place of blessing and usefulness. Are you in a place of brokenness? Do you need to be
        restored? Perhaps as a Christian you have done something wrong, and although you know God has forgiven you,
        you feel that God can no longer use you. What does Romans 11:29 say regarding this?

    b. Read 1 John 1:9. Why not pray right now asking God to forgive you, cleanse you and provide whatever it is you need
        (peace, encouragement, etc.) so that you may once again be used by God for His glory.

    c. Write 2 Corinthians 5:20 inserting your own name.

Nehemiah Lesson 13

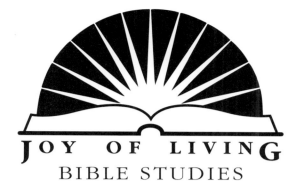

Preventing Burnout, Preserving Power

As we come to the closing study in this great book of Nehemiah it has been a refreshing thing for me to see how God greatly used this remarkable man, cup-bearer to the King of Persia, to restore the worship of Jehovah to the nation of Judah.

The title of this lesson: *Preventing Burnout, Preserving Power*, tells the whole story of Nehemiah's final acts. It is the account of his reform after his second return from Babylon to Jerusalem. It is the story, as we will see, of the reinstatement of Sabbath observances and his refusal to permit the intermarriage of Jews with pagan peoples. You might well be asking, "What does that all have to do with burnout and power?" I am glad you asked that! I will attempt to answer it as this passage unfolds.

Let us begin in Nehemiah 13 with verse 15, the restoring of the Sabbath regulations. Nehemiah says:

In those days I saw men in Judah treading winepresses on the Sabbath and bringing in grain and loading it on donkeys, together with wine, grapes, figs and all other kinds of loads. And they were bringing all this into Jerusalem on the Sabbath. Therefore I warned them against selling food on that day. Men from Tyre who lived in Jerusalem were bringing in fish and all kinds of merchandise and selling them in Jerusalem on the Sabbath to the people of Judah. I rebuked the nobles of Judah and said to them, "What is this wicked thing you are doing—desecrating the Sabbath day? Didn't your forefathers do the same things, so that our God brought all this calamity upon us and upon this city? Now you are stirring up more wrath against Israel by desecrating the Sabbath." (Nehemiah 13:15-18)

Even today in Israel you cannot get a hot meal in a Jewish hotel from sunset on Friday to sunset on Saturday. The elevators will not be operating. You must use the stairs to get to your room. The shops are closed. Buses quit running, all because it is the Sabbath. This causes a great deal of inconvenience to tourists. Even many Jews do not like it. But the orthodox Jewish groups are powerful enough that they can require the whole country to observe the Sabbath Day whether they like it or not.

Even in Nehemiah's day we can see that this was a burdensome requirement to the people. No work was to be done and no business to be carried out, making trade very inconvenient. On his return from Babylon, Nehemiah found that in the twelve years he was away people had begun again to ignore the Sabbath day requirements. The streets were full of traffic. The stores were wide open.

His reaction is one of shock, not so much at what was happening, because this had happened before, but at the ease with which the people seemed to forget the lessons of the past. He reminds them that this violation is a serious thing. "What are you doing?" he cries. "Don't you know that God takes the Sabbath seriously? All the hurt, calamity and disaster which we have been going through has been caused, according to the scripture, by the failure of our forefathers to observe the Sabbath regulations."

Nehemiah Orders Changes

Then, using his full authority as the governor, Nehemiah immediately orders some changes.

When evening shadows fell on the gates of Jerusalem before the Sabbath, I ordered the doors to be shut and not opened until the Sabbath was over. I stationed some of my own men at the gates so that no load could be brought in on the Sabbath day. Once or twice the merchants and sellers of all kinds of goods spent the night outside Jerusalem. But I warned them and said, "Why do you spend the night by the wall? If you do this again, I will lay hands on you." From that time on they no longer came on the Sabbath. Then I commanded the Levites to purify themselves and go and guard the gates in order to keep the Sabbath day holy. (Nehemiah 13:19-22a)

It is clear that Nehemiah was deeply concerned by this disregard of the Law. He saw it not merely as an ignoring of certain traditional ritual, but as something that God took very seriously. He is intent on trying to correct the difficulties that had caused so much of the problem of Israel in the past. So he orders the gates to be closed at sunset on Friday. Those who camped outside the walls, waiting for the regulations to be ended to come in and begin their selling, he orders driven away from the city. He does not want them even hanging around outside. He requires the

Levites to cleanse themselves and to guard the gates so that no one violates the Sabbath.

Then in a closing prayer in verse 22 Nehemiah humbly prays that God will guide him and bless him in this zealous concern and expression.

Remember me for this also, O my God, and show mercy to me according to your great love.
(Nehemiah 13:22b)

The Heart Of The Sabbath Is Rest

What does this all mean for us?

Should we also keep the Sabbath by refraining from work and travel? A lot of people today still think so.

In the highly honored film *Chariots of Fire,* Eric Liddell, the young Scottish athlete, refused to run a race on the Sabbath day because he had been brought up in the Presbyterian church to regard Sunday as the Sabbath. I think he was mistaken in that, but his actions are a wonderful picture of the teaching of the New Testament that "everything that does not come from faith is sin" (Romans 14:23). He would have violated his conscience had he not observed what he had been taught was right.

But as we have already seen throughout this book, these regulations imposed upon Israel, and these limitations, especially regarding the Sabbath, were what the New Testament calls "shadows," pictures of something even more important that God wants observed. God teaches that truth by means of these regulations, these pictures and shadows, but what He really wants is the truth they are portraying. And that truth, of course, is what the New Testament wants Christians to observe. You observe the Sabbath when you fulfill what the Sabbath portrays. What is that?

At the heart of the Sabbath is the word "rest." The Sabbath is intended for man, that he may learn to rest. Here is where the problem of burnout enters. We are a restless people today. One of the major problems everywhere is stress and burnout. People cannot handle life any more because of the tremendous pressures they are under.

I heard recently of a man who ran up to an airline office and said, "Give me a ticket." They said, "Where to?" He replied, "Anywhere. I've got business everywhere!" That is the kind of pressure that some have to live under these days.

The Sabbath, to put it in modern terms, is God's stress management program! It is how to prevent burnout — how to recover from too much pressure and catch up with yourself. It is how to gather yourself together, and become able to handle the work you must do, without falling apart or being emotionally damaged.

The first thing God emphasized in giving the Sabbath, of course, was that human bodies need rest. You cannot keep working day after day without exacting a tremendous toll on your body. Our bodies, even as believers, are not redeemed. They grow weary.

According to the Word of God the body must have one day in seven to rest. The mind and the emotions require it, too. We are under so much tension today from so many demands upon us that our emotions sometimes get out of joint. We find ourselves growing irascible, testy and short-tempered. We are unable to keep control at times. These are symptoms of approaching burnout. The spirit within, the very center of our being, requires time to meditate, to contemplate and relate to life. We need time to see the big picture and pull back for a bit from things around. God has provided for this in the Sabbath.

Two Reasons For The Sabbath

There are two reasons given in the scripture for the inauguration of the Sabbath. The first one is found in Exodus 20:11. There we are told that because God finished creation in six days, and at the end of the six days rested on the seventh day, He therefore asked His people to rest after six days of labor.

You have to ask yourself, why did God rest? God is not a man. He does not get weary. The answer is, He rested because He was through! He did what He intended to do. He accomplished His objective. What He is teaching by that is that man, too, must recognize a limit to his work. There is a time to say you are through. There is a need to let go, to stop, to allow the body, mind, and spirit to recognize its limitations, and be content with them.

The second reason the Sabbath was given is often ignored. It is found in Deuteronomy 5:15. God said to Israel, "Remember that you were slaves in Egypt and that the LORD your God brought you out of there with a mighty hand and an outstretched arm. Therefore the LORD your God has commanded you to observe the Sabbath day."

That is a different reason from that of creation. They were to rest in order to reflect on God's ability to work beyond the labors they had already completed. Israel did not deliver itself from Egypt. It could not. When they came to the Red Sea they panicked. They did not know how they were going to get through the waters. The Egyptian army was coming on like forty acres of horseradish behind them, and the Israelites were afraid. But God opened the waters before them. They were delivered with a mighty hand and an outstretched arm. Therefore, they were to think of that when they observed the Sabbath day, the day of rest.

Rest of Cessation

So there are two aspects of the Sabbath — creation and redemption. There are two forms of rest. There is a *rest*

Nehemiah Lesson 13

of cessation; a ceasing from our own works. As the much-loved old hymn has it,

Not the labors of my hands
Can fulfill Thy law's demands;
Could my zeal no respite know,
Could my tears forever flow,
All for sin could not atone;
Thou must save and Thou alone.

I cannot contribute to my own redemption. My good works do not save me, nor can they. That is the "rest" of the new creation. It is to cease from your own works and trust God in the work that He has done for you.

Rest of Regeneration

But then there is the rest of rejoicing in the mighty delivering power of God. That deliverance is a process. It goes on beyond the rest of salvation to the rest of accomplishment. It is learning how to keep calm and poised, to not become overwrought by anxiety or pressure but to keep steady because you are looking to God to work in what you are doing. That is a rest of faith in the mighty hand of God.

Jesus spoke of both of these in one wonderful sentence found in Matthew 11. "Come to me," He says, "all you who are weary and burdened, and I will give you rest" (Matthew 11:28). Just come, He says, that is all. "Come to me. Trust me. Rest upon what I have already done, and I will give you a rest." This is the rest of regeneration. We enter to become a new creation. Then He said, "Take my yoke upon you and learn from me [that is a process], ...and you will find rest for your souls" (Matthew 11:29). So there is a rest that is given and a rest that is found, as we walk on with the Lord.

Both of these are what God is concerned with in the Sabbath. This is what it seeks to picture. If we are doing these we are fulfilling the Sabbath as God intended it to be fulfilled. Stop your own work. Stop trying to save yourself. Trust His work for you. And then obey Him. Follow Him, learn of Him, accompany Him throughout your life. You will discover God working through you, doing mighty, delivering things which you could not do. That is the rest of accomplishment. Watch God at work!

It seems to me that the second aspect of rest is very little observed. We have a High Priest, the book of Hebrews says, in order that we may "approach the throne of grace with confidence, ... and find grace to help us in our time of need" (Hebrews 4:16). Very few people seem to rely upon that provision of strength and grace from on high to carry them through the pressures and the burdens of life.

God's Stress Management Program

Do you see now why I call the Sabbath God's stress management program? Burnout is overstress. We need to

stop and rest, and learn what God can do beyond what we have done.

I have learned in my own life to detect certain signs of stress. When I begin to get under the pile and feel anxious and pressured, I develop an itch in various places on my body. I have learned to recognize that immediately as a sign of stress. It cannot be cured with medicine, so I have trained myself to stop and take what I call "a mini-Sabbath." Let me suggest something to you. If you feel pressured at any time, try to get a half hour alone. That is about all you need.

Start with taking ten deep breaths to relax your physical body. Ask God to speak to you during this special time. Begin to review your life for the past few weeks: How much you have been driven? — The pressure of problems, and so on. Then ask God to help you put order and priority into your life. Take time to evaluate where you are spiritually. Make some new commitments. Write down those items that you feel are really important. Ask yourself, "If I only had a month to live, how would I spend my time?" Put your focus on God at work in your life. That is observing the Sabbath. That is God's stress management program.

The Final Problem

The final problem that Nehemiah faces was the tendency so common in Israel to ignore the prohibitions against intermarriage with pagan peoples. When he returned to Jerusalem, he found the people again disobeying the Law.

Moreover, in those days I saw men of Judah who had married women from Ashdod, Ammon and Moab. Half of their children spoke the language of Ashdod or the language of one of the other peoples, and did not know how to speak the language of Judah. (Nehemiah 13:23-24)

It was true then as it is today that when the fathers disobey, it is the children who suffer. These children were forgetting how to communicate in the language of Judah. Pagan tribes in the Old Testament portray the world and its ways of operation. The parallel in the church is very plain. When Christians begin to adopt the world's values and the world's ways, we invariably turn our children away from the things that make for stability and strength.

That is why Nehemiah is understandably upset by this. He takes drastic action.

I rebuked them and called curses down on them. [Literally, "I pronounced them cursed."] **I beat some of the men and pulled out their hair.** [I have been studying this as the way to handle a congregation that does not behave itself!] **I made them take an oath in God's name and said: "You are not to give your**

daughters in marriage to their sons, nor are you to take their daughters in marriage for your sons or for yourselves. Was it not because of marriages like these that Solomon king of Israel sinned? Among the many nations there was no king like him. He was loved by his God, and God made him king over all Israel, but even He was led into sin by foreign women. Must we hear now that you too are doing all this terrible wickedness and are being unfaithful to our God by marrying foreign women?"

One of the sons of Joiada son of Eliashib the high priest was son-in-law to Sanballat the Horonite. And I drove him away from me.
(Nehemiah 13:25-28)

This is, as I suggested in the last lesson, an Old Testament equivalent of Jesus cleansing the temple. I want to make clear that neither our Lord's action in the temple nor these actions by Nehemiah are a literal model of how Christians are to behave. We must never forget that these actions in the Old Testament are shadows. They are not something we are to repeat literally ourselves.

According to the New Testament, we are to move beyond the external teaching mechanism of the shadows to the meaning of what these shadows portray. It is the fulfillment of the shadow that is our model to follow. There is much difficulty in the world today because people have tried to carry these Old Testament restrictions over into today.

The struggle that occurred in South Africa over apartheid is a case in point. The Dutch people tried to take literally the requirements of the Old Testament to separate the races and to not allow their children to intermarry. That is the philosophy back of apartheid. The painful result is very visible in South African society today.

How are we to behave then? Here, Nehemiah portrays a commendable zeal in acting. He drives these people away because He was so offended by the fact that the grandson of the high priest had married the daughter of Sanballat the Horonite, the worshipper of the god Horon, who had opposed him when he first came to Israel to rebuild the wall. What are we to do today in fulfillment of this shadow?

This is a picture of the foolishness of trying to mix the world's ways and God's ways. That is what is portrayed by intermarrying with foreign women. God's work is to be done in God's way, and to borrow from the world is to introduce confusion into the camp.

Nehemiah's Prayer

There is an explanation of Nehemiah's concern and of his prayer in these closing verses.

Remember them, O my God, because they defiled the priestly office and the covenant of the priesthood and of the Levites.

So I purified the priests and the Levites of everything foreign, and assigned them duties, each to his own task. I also made provision for contributions of wood at designated times and for the firstfruits. (Nehemiah 13:29-31a)

And he closes his book with these words:

Remember me with favor, O my God.
(Nehemiah 13:31b)

The key here, of course, is these words, "because they defiled the priestly office and the covenant of the priesthood." The priestly office was to be a picture of the ministry of Jesus. He is the great High Priest who has come to meet man in his lostness and weakness and to restore him (see Hebrews 5:7-10). The church is called to the same work and the same ministry, as the Body of Christ.

Jesus Himself defined the work of the church for us in that wonderful scene in the synagogue of Nazareth where He quoted from Isaiah these words, "The Spirit of the Lord is on me, because he has anointed me to preach good news to the poor. He has sent me to proclaim freedom for the prisoners and recovery of sight for the blind, to release the oppressed, to proclaim the year of the Lord's favor" (Luke 4:18-19). That is the work of believers: to preach to people the good news of the gospel, to minister to people's hurts, to lift the burden of guilt in their lives, to teach them how to be free from sinful habits, how to oppose the powers of darkness and the occult world, to understand that God is in control of life, and to give hope to the hopeless. That is the work of the Christian, and that is always what suffers when the Christian begins to operate in the ways of the world.

I want to close by reading a brief quotation from John R. W. Stott who puts this very well. He says:

Our motive must be concern for the glory of God, not the glory of the Church or our own personal glory. Our message must be the good news of God, as given by Christ and His apostles, not the traditions of men or our own opinions. Our manpower must be the whole Church of God, and every member of it, not a privileged few who want to retain certain ministry as their own prerogative. Our dynamic must be the Spirit of God, not the power of human personality, or organization or eloquence. Without these priorities we shall be silent when we ought to be vocal.

So Nehemiah ends his book on a very practical note. This is the way Christians change the world. This is the way we affect the times in which we live. We are not here to be a tightly knit, quiet community, operating for our own benefit. We are here to change the world!